... a not very American perspective on
# Corporate Social Responsibility

Frode Nyeng

### ... a not very American perspective on
# Corporate Social Responsibility
## Responsibility for what?

Cappelen Akademisk Forlag

© J.W. Cappelens Forlag AS, Oslo 2007

Omslagsdesign: Graham Mansfield og Grete Foss
Sats: HS-Repro A/S
Trykk: Lobo Media as

ISBN 978-82-02-26408-6

Det må ikke kopieres fra denne boken i strid med åndsverkloven eller avtaler om kopiering inngått med KOPINOR, Interesseorgan for rettighetshavere til åndsverk. Kopiering i strid med lov eller avtale kan medføre erstatningsansvar og inndragning og kan straffes med bøter eller fengsel.

e-post: cafinfo@cappelen.no
http://www.cappelen.no

# Contents

Preface                                                                 9

**1** Freedom, responsibility and value
in economic life                                                       12

**2** Companies and social responsibility
A pragmatic perspective                                                53

**3** Business ethics
Economic calculations in the emotional landscape of ethics             81

**4** What is a company?
About value communities and value pluralism                           102

**5** Is economic reality growing?
More on economic power                                                134

**6** Summary and conclusion
Responsibility for what?                                              170

References                                                            177

*Cash flows towards efficiency and results, where results are equivalent to values that, again, are measured by cash — it is more or less a stroke of luck if the cash on its way should graze "The good" and "The beautiful". This is called National Wealth — a market that inexorably steer cash towards more cash.*

Peter Zoking

# Preface

I would not have written this book had it not been for the need, as I see it, to prevent the concept of social responsibility from being drained of ethical content[1] – a process that has been accelerated lately by the catchy, novel speech in business life. The continuously growing attention to so-called common values, ethical visions and value-based management is actually not very much about society – it is just more about the company. At the same time the use of unrealistic economic theories forces a wedge between the individual and the social community of society, a fact that increases the distance between the one who *has* responsibilities and what responsibility is *about*. Instead of talking about who has responsibility, we primarily need to discuss how we organize our society, taking care of the plurality of goods and social spheres needed for a rich human life. This is what social

---

[1] Three of the chapters in this book are rewritten, somewhat extended and adjusted versions of articles earlier published in Norwegian. Chapter 2 is based on the article "Bedrifter og samfunnsansvar – et pragmatisk perspektiv", *Magma – Tidsskrift for økonomi og ledelse*, no. 2, 2006. Chapter 3 is based on the article "Næringslivsetikk – besluttsomhetens kontra følsomhetens etikk", *Magma – Tidsskrift for økonomi og ledelse*, no. 3, 2002 and chapter 4 is based on the article "Hva er en bedrift? – et verdipluralistisk næringslivsetikkperspektiv", in *Frihet og mangfold – festskrift til Odd G. Arntzen*, Tapir Forlag, 2003.

responsibility is directed towards ensuring and improving. That is, we need to identify and discuss the mechanisms which determine this organisation; we need in this context to discuss power – economic power in a broad, discursive and symbolic sense.

Social responsibility is primarily about society. It is about money and profit as the source and means of the realization of other forms of value, about the limits of the market, about using the design of corporations as one possible way of organising our common responsibility to exploit our resources as efficiently as possible. It is about cash as a massive flow of opportunities to create a foundation for richer experiences and human growth. It should in other words not, for instance, be a discussion of whether the Nordic model of welfare can give our companies extra credibility and a push into the new global economy where social responsibility is demanded. If the society is the means and the company is the goal, the situation is turned upside down and the ethical content is really lost. Regardless of how decently the transactions are made in business life.

Hence the main line in this book is neither responsibility seen from the perspective of the company nor responsibility as I feel it should be attributed to the company. None of these questions can be discussed ethically unless we in advance take a closer look at the relations between companies and society as it is presented in economic theory. First of all we need to investigate how the important concepts of responsibility, value, welfare and freedom easily take on an economic sound – in other words how they are easily shaped by the power that lies in our economic thinking. Questions about social responsibility are closely related to the market as an institution, as a social practice where many of our needs, desires and goals are given legitimacy, and our thoughts about the good life are shaped in the culture of our time.

I want to express my thanks to my editor, Hilde Berit Kristoffersen, for enthusiastic support and for believing in this project from the very beginning, and to my colleague and friend Grete Wennes for critical reviews of the manuscript and valuable comments. I am most deeply grateful, again, to my dear wife Marit. Without her help, and most of all her unflagging support of my philosophical work, this book surely would not have been written.

Frode Nyeng
Trondheim, December 2006

Chapter 1

# Freedom, responsibility and value in economic life

My contention is that the company is not the appropriate arena for doing business ethics, and that the concept of CSR – corporate social responsibility – is a part of a rhetoric that actually covers up a wide range of important ethical challenges in economic life. The business company as we know it – typically as the public stock company – is a result of historical and social forces that in ethics should be subject to critical discussion. Even if ethical reflection and dialogue obviously have to be a part of everyday business, ethics will not gain any foothold until we open up the present framework of social organisation and ask fundamental questions about which goods will be appropriate for the market to handle and how business institutions are to be designed and related to each other. Only then can the ethical discussion show us real value questions, indicating the limits for economic thinking and the scope of the market, and at the same time stimulate our consciousness on the value of non-economic activities. In short, the place for economic values in life and society as a whole.

The arena for dialogue about social responsibility, therefore, has to be society itself – the political institutions, the educational organisations, the public hearings, the periodicals, newspapers and television, and for that matter also the pubs and the family gatherings. Any place where economic power dare show its face through arguments, where we can recognize how power works and challenge it in an open dialogical shaping and refinement of opinions. If we are to take responsibility in the role of employee and/or investor, we must first shape our sense of responsibility as a citizen. Ethics always reaches beyond social roles and sector-defined questions and problems. However, the fact that many companies today are of a size that makes their economies larger than the economies of many states represents a challenge when it comes to breaking out of the economic sphere as it is currently conceived, even when the topic is an ethical one. Inasmuch as we now find 50 companies and 50 states among the 100 largest economies in the world (measured in sales and GNP, respectively), debating the role of these selected corporations in such matters as taxation, human rights and environmental impact clearly is the most realistic approach to the subject. Nevertheless, economic power is not primarily connected to companies, not even large multinational corporations. It is connected to a widespread world of economic ideas and a certain view of human nature, which again is the more appropriate target of our critique.

## Core values or power criticism?

The core values of companies, established visions of corporate or "tribe" culture, value-based management policy and ethical rules of conduct, both on a company and a business sector level – they are all matters that in the current discussions are seen as concretizations of social responsibility. But the fact is that they are interpretations fundamentally shaped by economic power, as Lars Klemsdal points out: "The politically correct dogma that every motive – economic, human and social – can be joined in an optimal package solution, has become the the new bau flag of market liberalism."[2] And this is a power that ethics shall not spread or embellish, but has to challenge.

Actually, criticism of power in different shapes *is* the task and the content of ethics. Power, not only as it is manifested in a concentrated form by individuals, large groups of companies, distributors or consumer organisations, but as it resides in all of us, as members of a culture where economic thinking is obtaining a dominant position. It is all about gaining a critical view on this, often invisible, power that is woven into our array of values, our goals of life and our image of reality – to identify the assumptions we take for granted and which are governing us by shaping our reality, or lifeworld. To awaken and ascribe responsibility is first of all a matter of raising consciousness towards one's own, often silent thoughts and attitudes, which create the practical context for the recognition of our problems. Taking an ethical attitude means that no values are protected against discussion.

Therefore we can not view corporate social responsibility as something rooted in companies organized in a given economic system, or that taking such responsibility is to be accounted for based on established measures and criteria for success. These will basically be the capitalistic criteria of growth and profit. It is not at all given that all companies will or should show social responsibility in order to gain further profit. But, as we shall see, we should not take for granted that there exists such a strict and necessary contrast between ethics and profit either, that it is social responsibility only when it actually costs. For at bottom, what we really are discussing here is how to unite economic and non-economic considerations in the good life, both at the community and the personal level.

Applying different logics of action depending on whether we are talking about money or morals is highly misleading. Money and pro-

---

[2] Klemsdal (2004, p. 118). My translation from Norwegian.

fit have to be understood as beneficial and as an expression of freedom of action at the same time as our moral reflection has to make it responsible. That is: give qualitative, value-based boundaries for the accumulation of money and profit-seeking behaviour. And when we create qualitative boundaries for profit and the market, it is not really appropriate to say that it "costs". What we do in our ethical efforts is to make strong, value-based evaluations that establish other measures for evaluation of certain goods. It would not be proper to say that prohibiting billboards in city parks "costs" lost advertising income, since what we actually are doing is defending public spaces where all people can meet freely and without commercial pressure. And the fact that a park is open to everybody, without any demand for payment, is exactly what constitutes one of its benefits.

Ethics is therefore primarily about what we can accept as relevant measures for value creation and good performance, and not about companies having to produce "extra value" for the society they are operating in. A concept of social responsibility that does not challenge the dominant construction of a purely quantitative measure of value creation lacks ethical substance. It is all about how to create good economic solutions for the citizens of a society, and that these solutions must be viewed within the perspective of the whole life of the citizens. This will of course have to be seen in the light of the actual resource and value challenges that have evolved, problems that partially are results of growth-based economic development itself. Incorporated as *a part of* an economic practice based on profit as the core motive, ethics has narrow boundaries. It will often not be ethics at all, but strategy. But ethics can not have hidden agendas; it needs to be able to ask the uncomfortable and unprofitable questions about our basic assumptions of what promotes, and what hampers, real freedom, value and welfare in our time. An important part of what we in this regard have to challenge, is why the free market and continuous economic growth often is presented as something almost natural, connected to human nature itself, as the basis upon which all other ways of common action must be evaluated and substantiated.

Is it, for instance, obvious that we really want to have a free market when it comes to choosing primary schools for our children, if such a possibility will result in a loss in other values, such as children developing fellowship across social classes, and considerable differences between the schools with respect to the quality of the education they can offer? A real value question is this: can education actually be considered primarily a private good at all? Or would it be better to accept it as a process of cultural refinement, a genuinely common good where people are closely connected in mutual development, and a process that consequently will suffer if we accept a state where persons understand themselves as individual actors with their own "demand for knowledge" (later to be redeemed in competition advantages in working life). We can not talk about social responsibility without at the same time being aware of the social values that are to be considered responsibly – and what ways of organizing are the most appropriate in order to sustain the diversity of values that we want. Another evident example of this: if at least some of the art that is produced is supposed to give us images that we dislike and that challenge our desires, "products" that actually pull us out of the known and dear, it can hardly be produced only based on our willingness to pay.

In this book I therefore will not focus on how one as a manager or employee in a company should grasp social responsibility. Such action should, by the way, always be evaluated and negotiated with sensibility and a close eye to the actual situation. My concern is more directed towards how we understand and assess the relation between economic practice and the rest of social life, and how this understanding can give the concept of social responsibility genuine ethical content. We need to prevent misuse of the concept of ethics. Ethics should be reserved for the reflections that really challenge our predominant thoughts, reflections that make us conscious of the thoughts that often are connected to a given view of human nature and society. It can be difficult to grasp facts that we take for granted, that what we take to be natural and universally valid might be historically contingent and culturally shaped. In our time there is the notion that the market generally and universally is what will secure all good – and that divergences from market solutions mean that resources are not optimally exploited. What we might call market fundamentalism is spreading a wide array of such assumptions — that private (wealth, initiative, solutions) will always be better than public (wealth, initiative, solutions) and that almost everything can be fairly traded in a market. Social responsibility can not be ethical without first conducting a close investigation of this major direction of the development of our society.

Little reflection is necessary to understand that increasing commercial pressure on children, and exporting industrial production to countries with less strict environmental regulations are, to put it mildly, ethically dubious. It takes greater reflection to enable us to expose how our goal-directed economical choices might undermine our ability to be genuinely present in fragile social situations outside economic life, or how our eye for the totality of nature is impaired by the fact that we are trained to evaluate it piece by piece and sectioned into resources that again create added value by economic standards. Or that a proclamation announcing that cultural life should be steered in the direction of what "most people" want, will omit that what people want is not given once and for all, and that the legitimacy of cultural life might lay in the fact that it challenges, extends and refines people's opinions and values. Little or nothing of such evaluations is allotted space in the ethical work within the companies. Still, it is in such confrontation with different values that social responsibility will obtain both its shape and its content.

## Atomism or holism?
## A key question in economic ethics

My understanding of these thematics is marked by my opinion that ethical analysis of economic activity has to be coupled with a critical attitude towards economic theory, towards theoretical models and their basic assumptions and views of what it is to act as a human being. In the economic area it is not far from theory to practice. For, as presented in the Danish book *Kritik af den økonomiske fornuft (Critique of Economic Reason)* "The science of economics has to acknowledge and come to terms with the fact that it is also a practical subject. Economic theorizing has a fundamental influence on social reality and shapes our self-understanding as economic or non-economic actors."[3]

The retroactive force of theories has to be taken seriously. This is a point that we also know from the philosophy of science, from the well-known criticism of positivism in the social sciences during the 1960s and -70s. Criticism raised by, among others, the Norwegian philosopher Hans Skjervheim, who insisted on the connection between the theory of science, ethics and assumptions regarding human nature. Economic theory as a social science has to be a part of the society that it describes. Economists can not, therefore, conduct their research from the perspective that they can neutrally describe the society from the outside. They have to consider that they are participating in society and that the knowledge they produce can influence the actions and connections that constitute economic practice. Economic theory may not be a full-blown view of life, but nor is it just a neutral, analytical device. Quite a lot of research has also been done in recent years on the different ways economic theory and economic language can become self-fulfilling. Theory is describing soci-

---
[3] Fenger-Grøn/Kristensen (2001, p. 15). My translation from Danish.

ety more and more as an economic reality inhabited by rational egoists and structured by organisations designed on assumptions about opportunistic behaviour, because economic actors understand and adjust themselves and their actions in the light of economic theory.[4]

Criticism of theory will therefore be closely connected to the practical action in this field. This is evident if we for instance take a closer look at our understanding of how economic actors are related to one another. This is a core question when we discuss how power can be identified and how social responsibility can be anchored in practice through open dialogue between different parties. It is relatively easy to conclude that the traditional, and still dominant, economic theory will yield a picture where both power and dialogue are absent or just marginal phenomena.

Economic practice is, according to such theory, composed of separated, utility-maximising parts connected to each other by laws and regulations, what we usually refer to as external connections. According to the theory, economic actors behave like social atoms that live their lives without real – that is to say, emotional, linguistic and identity-sensitive – relations to others. It is all about adjusting to costs determined by the competitive situations. The theory gives us a mechanical picture of the world, where individual actors are easily replaced and where coordination of action is achieved mainly through prices and formal contracts. In such a world no one is superior to another, and development will be according to laws defined by economy. The goals are given, and rationality is consequently purely a technical-instrumental rationality, which is possible only when weak, external links exist between actors. This is of course an idealised and "non-realistic" picture, but still a picture that shapes the foundation for a wide range of decisions that are being made

---

[4] See Ferraro/Pfeffer/Sutton (2005) for an excellent overview.

about the scope and manner of operation of the market, which again shapes our attitudes toward market solutions. Thus the picture is not an innocent, theoretical simplification.

An alternative model depicts economic actors not as social atoms, but as parts of an organic, social whole, connected through a wide range of relations of power and ways of communication, together with the use and protection of common resources. Such a social holism, where everybody is what they are through the type and strength of their relations, their meetings, and the way they approach and defend their values, is characterised by a communicative and emotional attachment to different communities of various size. Relationships between the actors are then basically, and from the start, characterised by a profound mutual responsibility – which means that one can not justify actions by referring to external conditions or a systemic orderliness, but must demonstrate that they are reasonable and meaningful through strong evaluations. Value creation is not a result of profitability alone, but rather accompanies a broad range of communicative interaction between all affiliated parties. Interactions where different standards of values are established and where free choice includes taking a moral point of view, not simply consideration of one's own positive freedom, but also freedom of everybody else.

This, too, is of course a simplification, an idealisation, and a conventionalised picture, but it deviates from the atomistic picture by trying to anchor theory in ontology, in an explicit view of human nature, and it is therefore closer to the complexity that characterises being a human being. Standard economic theory does not start with ontology; it does not start with fundamental considerations of human beings and society at all. It starts with conventional assumptions, and this makes it possible to cultivate a view where self-interest – often narrowly and materialistically interpreted – represents the true nature of mankind. In the holistic picture, people are so closely bound together through norms, traditions and different forms of communicative action, that such a cultivation is impossible.

Thus the alternative model yields a picture where individuals can not exist outside the complex of social interconnections. The individual and the collective are not antagonisms, but shape each other mutually, and speaking of collectives is not speaking of a strangling collectivism. It is, however, easy to end up with such conclusions when we start out with typical economic actions shaped by our institutions, such as wage and price negotiations, where parties are pitted against each other. But, as we will also see in Chapter 4, it is possible to see this conflictual and competitive element in a wider perspective, where cooperation is also one of the basic economic principles. The general philosophical point here is that the technical rationality will always be part of a larger cultural context – it is inevitably incorporated in *institutions* in a broad sense (as, for instance, making promises, marriage, a lecture and national holidays are all social institutions). This is how economic actions can create profit which contributes to a rich life in a community, and only by that can they become meaningful.

Still, it can be claimed that large actors in economic practice are increasingly giving life to the first picture, that they see themselves as disconnected from society, as creating value for themselves (or their so-called owners) rather than administering a part of society's resources - an administration that would carry with it a wide spectrum of duties and qualifications for the freedom of economic action. One indication of such a development is that large companies are increasingly run with a view to the stock market, which again means more short-term planning and obviously a narrower horizon when it comes to values taken into account on their own premises. Ethically this is deeply problematic, because the assertion that the job of managers is to maximize shareholder value simply lacks convincing justification.

According to, among many others, Bent S. Tranøy, it can be justifiably stated that this signifies a growing self-understanding for these companies. They perceive themselves as free from any larger contract with the society.[5] They are, as they see it, atoms floating free in society, units that follow "the laws of the market" within given legal regulations, and without links to local connection, history and mutual interaction with the surroundings. In this we see a determinism that obviously has to be defeated before we can develop an ethical understanding of social responsibility. It has to be defeated – even if this kind of narrow decision horizon might be said to have a substantial basis in the history of ideas and without doubt can be said to define the modern understanding of the economic actor.

## The modern understanding of what it is to be human – and of the economy

Let me here briefly sketch how self-interest finds its place as the moral heart of economy: theories stating that the actual nature of the human being consists of acting according to self-interest are in our time willingly given a evolutionistic justification. But if we step back and take a glance at the situation before evolutionary biology, we can find a corresponding, naturalistic understanding of the human being as a covetous being essentially governed by its natural urges. This is an understanding fundamental to the view of ethics and morality that characterizes our modern era, where the individual is the centre (the source of morals is also to be found within the human being itself) and where the primary human impetus is to provide for oneself and one's family.

If we follow the early modern development of continuously growing trade and production of goods, and finally the modern capital-

---

[5] See Tranøy (2006, p. 247–249). My translation from Norwegian.

istic markets, we find that its history is joined together with a consolidated idea of trade and competitive economic activity as morally doubtful. We also see that this kind of activity slowly gains legitimacy by being interpreted as a relatively less harmful (compared with real war) and gradually socially beneficial effect of a martial and covetous human nature. But activity oriented towards making money has never been meant to take care of the whole human being and dominate entire societies. Differentiating the economic and financial activities from the rest of society was supposed to contain the consequences of selfish and socially destructive forces. When we now, in our time, try to (re)create and attend to society as a whole by using a concept of corporate social responsibility, we should be reluctant to do so solely on the basis of the driving forces of the market, forces that for a long time have been considered as creating effective solutions from a fundamentally amoral principle of competition rather than from co-operation and a feeling of community.

According to this modern understanding, the human being is not completely without sympathy and moderation, but it is dominated by its striving to meet its own demands — or as the classicist Adam Smith puts it, "the great affair" is acquisitiveness and the demand for money. The natural horizon of the decisions of a human being is himself and those nearest to him. The modern challenge therefore becomes putting the natural desires of each individual into a system and doing this in a way that can be beneficial for the whole, that is, society in general, rather than working on the impossible task of changing human nature. A basic tenet of the philosophy of Adam Smith's time was, as mentioned, that "war" in trade and economy was preferable to war as we know it in a military sense. Protecting your own interests had to be and could be transformed into a productive force, a force that secured the welfare of the society. Or as the slogan says: "personal vices become public virtues". To imagine an extensive social responsibility as something all economic actors have and can claim – consequently by both individuals and companies – is, viewed in this context, a departure from the modern ideas of individualism and personal autonomy that led to capitalistic economy.

Greed, covetousness and desire for money have a long historical tradition of being morally condemned, but, as pointed out, these forces have at the same time been made the core power of economy and by that the power of social development. It is important for our understanding of capitalistic economy that we do not let this central point slip out of view. When Adam Smith, in 1776 with his monumental work *The Wealth of Nations*, expressed the theoretical-ideological foundation of modern market economy, it was exactly in the shape of a systematization of self-interest and desire for money. His radical declaration was that once the rules of the game are established, society is best served by leaving all actors to act for their own benefit. This is what we may call the modern dichotomising of economic ethics: on one level covetousness is put into the system in such a way that the individual striving for its own gain will also result in the best output for society (this is what we, and Adam Smith himself, refer to by the well-known expression, *the invisible hand*). On another level this atomistic activity is controlled and limited through laws and public regulations (what we may call the hand of politics).

## Profit and the whole individual

Milton Friedman is possibly the most well-known advocate of a liberalistic view of companies founded on such an understanding of economic ethics. Under assumptions of perfect competition it can be claimed that an individual company's social responsibility corresponds perfectly to its economic responsibility. That is presuming we base our views on the economic view of the human being that has been sketched here. The title of Friedman's classic article on this topic is 'The Social Responsibility of Business Is to Increase its

Profits", which, it must be said, is straight to the point. Friedman's conclusion in this article is a phrase that must be one of the most quoted in this discipline:

> .....in a free society... there is one and only one social responsibility of business – to use its resources and engage in activities designed to increase its profits so long as it stays within the rules of the game...[6]

In other words, it is an explicit denial of any role of ethical considerations in management practice. Friedman's main argument for this assumption is clearly based on the previously mentioned dichotomy of economic ethics, and it is basically this: it is unambiguously a political task to decide in such matters as tax and allocation of welfare goods. Once the *rules of the game* are politically approved, a company should be engaged in its primary task which is maximising its internal goals in the market. If a company undertakes "social duties" beyond this, it will imply an unfortunate mix of roles, of the role of the individual human being as manager of the company or employee and the political role of the individual on the other hand. According to Friedman the relationship between a human being as an economic actor and as a political or moral subject can be seen as a sheer division of labour – accordingly with regard to different roles on the same practical level.

A completely different interpretation of this relationship is given by Learned, Dooley and Katz in another article on the relation between "personal values and business decisions", an interpretation that at least in some parts corresponds to the holistic understanding of ethics and responsibility that I am trying to sketch here:

---

[6] Friedman (1970, p. 45).

> ... the very fact that the businessman, first of all, is a man. As a man, he shares the universal trait of wanting to be certain that his life has meaning and purpose... the businessman inevitably finds himself in a state of inner conflict... Like all men, the businessman inevitably returns to the question of ultimate values and to the question of whether his total life is serving those values in the way he would wish.[7]

Discussing the relationship between the human being in business life and the human being as ethically and politically involved in society is something completely different from discussing division of labour. We can put it like this: the human-being-in-the-company and the-human-being-as-a-moral-actor can be seen as two different personae only as long as we take for granted that the company is only and fully an economic unit – companies actually exist only to serve the economic interests of the shareholders. But as I have stated previously, my contention will have to be that it is the duty of ethics to criticise such a view of the company and of this narrowness of economic life in general. The human being as an employee and the human being as a moral actor can only be regarded as "two alternative roles", as Friedman claims, if we see the human being in an *already defined* economic reality. But in ethics we actually put it the other way around; we put the whole human being in the centre and see economic action as one of its (possible) ways of acting.

Freidman's view can be criticised as "economism". And we can state that this is a critique with two fronts. First of all we can indicate how the world has changed and that the responsibility of the economic actors has to be reconsidered in a new and wider manner than during the growth of capitalism. Today it is no longer only – and maybe not even primarily – the autonomy and independence of

---

[7] Learned/Dooley/Katz (1959, p. 82).

the individual that is threatened and needs protection. It can equally be claimed to be our common conditions of life, of both an ecological and cultural nature: the biodiversity, the climate, the diversity of cultures and ways of assessment, the global justice, and not least, the social dignity of weak and exploited groups of the world's human population. Yet, to claim that all of these circumstances can be rolled into the price mechanism, such that the markets can correct and limit themselves towards the right solutions, is built, mildly stated, on very unrealistic assumptions.

Secondly, and more principally, we can criticize the underlying naturalistic view of the human being. We can state that the human being is a historical, cultural and self-interpreting ("hermeneutic") being whose nature will change depending on the ways it understands itself. There is accordingly nothing universally true about the thesis that we are egoists striving for as much as possible for ourselves. This is rather a historically contingent way for us to interpret our actions, and besides, as Ferraro, Pfeffer and Sutton point out: "A growing body of evidence suggests that self-interested behavior is learned behavior, and people learn it by studying economics and business."[8] It is course naive to believe that human beings, as biological creatures, do not have a tendency to provide for themselves as best they can, but it is just as unrealistic to assume that we are incapable of reflecting more deeply and in richer terms on what forms our behaviour, on the values we strive for and respect.

As whole human beings we always possess the ability to go beyond what we actually strive for and look for different possibilities. Or as Erik Lundestad states: "To simply appreciate something is to lack knowledge of what it actually will lead to or what place it has in our lives... If what we appreciate is to have normative power, if it is to commit us and be something we support, it presumes that it is

---

[8] Ferraro/Pfeffer/Sutton (2005, p. 14).

subject to an evaluation."⁹ At this point it is also necessary to mention that when it comes to Adam Smith, his views of human beings were much richer and more complex than sketched here, and for that matter than in much economic literature.¹⁰

If we take this seriously, we will see that the most interesting area for ethical discussion will be the social space we live in *between* state and market. A room that does not matter in the duplex ethical scheme above and which economic theory rarely discusses to any degree worth mentioning.

## The space between state and market

Accordingly, my key statement will be that social responsibility can not be defined and handled by companies with certain goals. This applies to the whole organisation of society – and it is primarily the responsibility of the citizens, human beings as a whole, not economic actors. The basis for all discussion about social responsibility has to be our experience of the relationship to other citizens as a real community, and consequently that a viable civil society exists, a society where we are able to discuss and assess the role of the economy in the community. If not, we will rather have to talk about an extended

---

⁹ Lundestad (2006, unpublished). My translation from Norwegian.

¹⁰ The literature on the philosophy of Adam Smith is extensive, and the interpretations of his views on human beings are diverse. A short and interesting interpretation, quite contrary to the current, economic understanding of his theory on human beings as governed by self-interest, can be found in *On Ethics and Economies* written by Nobel prize winner Amartya Sen (1987, p. 22–28). Here Sen claims that economists often neglect the complex ethical analysis of emotions and behaviour Smith performed and at the same time exaggerate his defence of choices based on self-interest alone. The latter defence is by Sen thought to be limited to defined, economic contexts alone. In Smith's philosophy, according to Sen, sympathy with others and strong self-discipline are generally vital ingredients in good behaviour.

*economic* responsibility, a responsibility for making profit-seeking behaviour decent, a concept that does not question economic goals, development and growth itself.

Therefore, with an eye toward social responsibility, we can not just search for the mechanisms behind market solutions; in addition we have to move into a more open, normative room where we can question whether the market solutions are ethically good. We can not just record that salaries for top executives are defined in the free market, as legal agreements between independent parties and that by that all necessary formal terms are granted. The pay is not, thereby, necessarily good from an ethical point of view. We have to ask if we feel that it is a positive development within society that top executive salaries, for instance in the USA, during the last 25 years has increased relative to that of the average employee from 50:1 to 500:1. We need to ask what consequences this may have for social security, the feeling of community, the possibilities for dialogue, for empathy and for the interpretation of the conditions of the good life.

Though as long as the economic actors understand themselves more or less as actors playing in a closed economic game, we will not find such problems anchored in open dialogue between the involved parties – corporations, managers, employees, authorities, citizens. We can not settle for this as a development following naturally from the economic ideas, ideas that may seem reasonable from a purely theoretical point of view. We can, for example, ask as the Swedish writer Göran Rosenberg does in his book, *Plikten, profitten og kunsten å være menneske (Duty, Profit and the Art of Being Human)*[11]: how is society possible when human beings apprehend themselves as independent from society? When we chisel out a reasonable relation between our role in business life and our social responsibility, it has to be with a view to the common formation of thought and attitude. Turning a critical

---

[11] Rosenberg (2005).

eye to the consequences of the actions of the individual actors in the market "as it actually is functioning", is not enough.

Still, much of what is taught in economic education is based on the rather pessimistic view that human beings most naturally will relate to each other in a calculating and egoistic way. Even when following norms and value-based convictions, we are taught, it is because of something else, something non-moral; out of fear of sanctions, or fear of failing in the eyes of the others, to create an image or to enjoy the feeling of appearing to be good and noble. Economic actors do not even behave reflexively with respect to laws and regulations. They rather just calculate the risk of being revealed, the possible size of the penalty and social condemnation and base their considerations on breaking or meeting the regulations on this basis. In this way theft, for instance, can seriously be considered harmful only because it may reduce productivity; justice can be considered important primarily because it leads to the avoidance of waste.[12] Besides, this is how ethical utility theory often is interpreted in economics (one simply seems to "forget" the genuinely social dimension in the original philosophical utilitarianism, the principle of respect for *overall* or *everybody's* utility and welfare). But this is clearly a perverted liberal way of thinking, a thinking that let the social way of life disappear behind instrumental considerations.

Economic theory therefore also shows us a questionable tension between state and market. First of all we have to emphasize that the relationship between state and market represents a much more complex and differentiated interaction between politics and economic development than the theory shows. But, as indicated, it is in itself a confusing theoretical line of demarcation, because as citizens people act towards each other in a number of ways in the space *between* state and market. What is important here is what we call our lifeworld,

---

[12] Ghoshal (2005).

which consists of our plurality of ways of understanding situations and of seeking meaning that neither exists in high level politics nor acts of trade or consumption. In between the free choice of the individual and the individual controlled by the government we find the rich, multi-faceted social life that shapes our values and makes us what we truly are. These are social and cultural arenas of meaning construction that include norms, schemes of interpretation and habitual action that we only partly are explicitly aware of, but that truly create the basis of all experiences.

So what is the point in bringing this aspect of social life into this discussion? Well, the economic thesis that we primarily behave in a results-oriented way towards each other presupposes tacitly such a social and cultural basement. It is only through shared interpretations that situations can arise where something actually is at stake for the individual, problems where we also *can* behave in a results-oriented manner and eventually solve them by calculating the best alternative. Therefore the space between state and market is a web of assumptions and social, practical and moral connections that we all take for granted (our lifeworld) and of different arenas for dialogue and development of non-economic realization of value (what we normally speak of as the civil society).

We can put it like this: while the lifeworld is the symbolic dimension of culture that forms the background of our problems, making them the kind of problems they are, it is in the civil society that we actually act as citizens, probing into the situations we find ourselves in, often in the common effort of solving problems. If we push the market and the economic sense up front as the "most natural" arena for acting and problem solving, we both fail to see its premises and risk reducing our possibilities for responsibility.

## The market as a standard

It is worth remarking that the original meaning of profit is something charitable, something that brings us forward. However, if we are to comprehend this phenomenon we need to move far beyond the prevailing meaning of profit and other central economic notions. Consequently, if discussing social responsibility is to extend and enrich our sense of reality, we need to challenge the idea of calculating behaviour as an expression of human nature and the market as the dominating arena for value creation.

But it is easier to have opinions, write, think and act within the ruling paradigm – a paradigm where the market as an institution defines central practical notions such as freedom of choice, value, efficiency and welfare. What we need to remember is that these are notions with a particularly long and complex history, notions that can be traced back to competing philosophical positions. Therefore it should not be *easy* for us to use these notions when we are occupied with economic ethics. The task of philosophy is, also in these matters, to create resistance in our thinking. Though the simplifications that, among others, are made in the theory of welfare economy make it easy – too easy. The American philosopher Elisabeth Anderson has pointed this out as a problem with circularity in definitions:

> ... the conception of human good embraced by welfare economics. It defines a person's welfare as the satisfaction of her given preferences, which it conceives as automatically expressed in her choices ... This conception of welfare is tailored to present markets in their best light.[13]

When welfare is so closely attached to preferences, and preferences

---
[13] Anderson (1993, p. 166).

are claimed to be revealed through actual choices, the solutions of the market necessarily will have to come out well – thus the market in a cultivated form responds to action, and not to value-based arguments ("exit not voice", as economists like to say). In this we also find a circular argument of justice that can be expressed thus: the market rewards talent, effort and skills, and the talented, willing and skilled are defined as the winners in the competition of the market. Therefore, the solutions of the market are always judged as right, even if the solutions themselves are part of the definition of what is right.

For those who do not ask any deep questions, we here will have a great deal of "traps of thoughts". For, as Anderson points out: the market is an institution that responds to people's wishes, while "...an ideal democracy distributes goods in accordance with public principles, not in accordance with unexamined wants"[14]. As citizens of society we find values, principles and goals through "voice" – through reflection, communication and joint action. Economic efficiency will first of all not always be promoted by the free market and, more importantly here, such efficiency is not always what we really want to promote. Besides, the dynamics of our society are such that any gains in efficiency only add to more profit, which again is realized in new investments and results in growing consumption. It is a part of the system that it shall grow on its own terms. Judged on the basis of market standards it is far from certain that this will always be profitable in the deeper sense – that it is bringing us forward as human beings. With substantiated "public principles" it is far from certain that we reach the same conclusion.

If we view economy from a wider social science and humanistic position, the "core" of the sphere can be read as a rather narrow understanding of rational action. If we want to view economy as a

---

[14] Anderson (1993, p. 159).

concept of social responsibility, the goal has to be to open up a wide and critical professional discussion. But this also presupposes that we do not remain in the perspective of management, but widen the discussion to view social responsibility in a real social perspective.

## The management versus a social perspective

There is no doubt which perspective dominates and has the greatest influence in shaping the concept of corporate social responsibility (CSR). CSR has its origin in Anglo-American business life and management literature and is consequently shaped as a tool for management, without challenging the basic forces of economic life. It is rather quite the contrary: the understanding built into it is that in order to make money one has to act in accordance with a public increasingly focusing on other things than money. Ethics reaches companies filtered, not through a critical system but through a moderating public that demands honesty and transparency in order to *secure and preserve* the advantages of the system. Viewed from this perspective, CSR is a movement in the direction of ethical capitalism, trade based on legitimate interests and expectations between economic actors. This can be appreciated as a more decent economic practice, or at the same time be disliked as a cover of ethical problems attached to capitalism as a social system.

Nevertheless, any ethical concept of social responsibility calls for one taking a perspective of the society that can make clear whether its organisation is commendable – if it is constituted by institutions that are acknowledged as valuable, and that the division of labour between these can be accepted as rational in a deep sense. The concept of responsibility should be defined with a view to companies as *in principle* an integrated part of social life. In other words, it should be based on ideas of the good society and a thorough understanding of the social challenges that we currently face and which are now cropping up in public discussions. CSR activities in companies should be based neither on a need to control, nor on the fear of the negative impact of loss of branding value or failing sales.

All companies have, of course, a responsibility towards their employees, lenders, owners and customers – that is: a responsibility for the interest these parties put in their relationship with the company. Such stakeholder-relations are given a lot of attention in the literature on social responsibility and business ethics. As a concretization of the diversity of the interest that the company manages, and for pointing out that stock owners are but one group among the many contributors to a company's resources, this is a good model. But related to the concept of social responsibility and as a basis for overall analysis of power and value, it fails to be complete. We are in danger of discussing a narrow definition of diversity, a diversity of interests that all focus towards their interpretation of one goal, namely self-interest without any genuine social dimension built into it.

At this point we need to be aware of the fact that *to organise* in general can be said to imply disclaimer of responsibility. This might be a strange thought, but it becomes significant when we remember that organising is structuring, which again means to arrange social life in accordance with certain ways of problem solving – and thereby with certain modes of problem recognition. And by giving some perspectives precedence, other perspectives of reality are omitted. It is with this as background that we in Chapter 5 will take a closer look at economic power. Organisation and responsibility ethically require people that are able to grasp the totality, that are not completely absorbed by organisations and the ways of problem solving structured within them. Commitment to honesty, integrity and "dignity in the role" as a manager or employee can be said to close or at least slow down the possibility of a real consciousness of value and construction of meaning.

This means that the social perspective should not be seen as a part of the management perspective even if this is often attempted in the literature. In the award-winning book *Företaksetik (Business Ethics)*, by Tomas Brytting, we find the following statement:

> Based on a view of the human being that emphasizes our individual *and* social nature, our material *and* existential needs, the main task of business ethics is to help managers and employees of companies to take *individual responsibility for the common good*.[15]

This may seem both obvious and harmless in all its simplicity. But as said earlier: companies are meant to be organised in such a way that the people working there can forget about operating based on any concept of "common good". So what we primarily need is not managers and employees that through extraordinary achievements are able to take individual responsibility for the common good in the economy. What we need are human beings that as citizens are able to put their economic roles in perspective and see their economic goals in connection to non-economic values. This is the only way social responsibility can advance us as educated and mature persons.

And here we have a basic point that explains why we can not easily define freedom and welfare with respect to how the (idealized) market works. It is perhaps somewhat simplified, but we can claim that this is where we find the border between liberal and (market) liberalistic thought – in the comprehension of educated autonomous actors. This can be illustrated with an example based on education, as mentioned earlier: commitment to a good public education system is best understood as stemming from a liberal rather than a liberalistic ideology. The basis is that we can not just assume that people will grow up to be autonomous masterful decision makers, but that society has to make sure that they do. And this can be done by limiting

---

[15] Brytting (1999, p. 11). My translation from Swedish.

the use of the market as a solution in areas that deal with the pragmatic assumptions of a well-functioning market economy, among these the development of knowledge and refinement of the concept of value.

However, in a liberalistic market perspective knowledge is also an individual factor and, thereby, an economic good, which gives us the opportunity to focus on this division as follows: for companies, what matters is obtaining and using knowledge in order to provide for economic growth and to influence people with the purpose of gaining profit. In a liberal perspective of society what primarily matters is letting knowledge form a part of an open, democratic dialogue about the development of society. We see that the division is between an instrumental aspect and an aspect of refinement. In liberal thinking we can not merely assume, as we can in the less complex variants of market liberalism, that persons quite simply are educated and autonomous with a good view of how society works. A part of social responsibility lies in securing and protecting the social areas where the autonomy and its underlying prerequisite of critical thinking can be practised and kept alive. If everything is interpreted as "a factor of the economy" (in the same way as research and higher education more and more often are reportedly the most important factors in the competitive power of the country) responsibility will indeed have poor conditions.

This is an urgent practical dilemma between two basic perspectives of knowledge and shows that scientific knowledge has to include what we traditionally note as enlightenment and refinement. That we, in short, as whole human beings have to make sure that we are not hit by the poverty in concepts and perspectives that organising strictly in accordance with economic principles may create. This picture also includes what the Norwegian philosopher Gunnar Skirbekk describes as "the problem in the debate about consumer society and the relationship between genuine and not genuine goods and needs, and about wishes that primarily are manipulated and not real."¹⁶ In other words: in a liberal perspective there is room for what we often call ideology criticism, demonstration of false consciousness and need of awareness, while this often will be stamped as quite simply paternalism within a liberalistic framework. This last comment will be further discussed in Chapter 5.

## Loyalty, responsibility and the rules of the game

Parallel to the hard dynamics of constant readjustment that characterizes many companies trying to cope with complex surroundings, management is defined – at least in theory – as increasingly wider, softer and more democratic. Slogans like value-based management, usually with a view to the whole human, are often used. In particular the emotional attachment each individual develops in identification with the organisation, is put on the agenda alongside rational reasoning and the practical skills. This can be seen as a very praiseworthy dimension in creating an inclusive work life and in stimulating social responsibility, but on the other hand it represents a frightening conception of the human being where employment is elevated to the one and only real means of value creation and self-realisation (and this we will challenge in the next chapter). In addition, these efforts in creating a feeling of attachment and membership support a demand for loyalty.

Yet while "everything changes" and "employees just have to accept more insecurity", partly because in the light of management's primarily serving stockholders' interests, employees are treated more and more often as a casual, replaceable resource, employers nevertheless demand an even greater degree of employee loyalty . This applies

---

[16] Skirbekk (2005, p. 117).

in both the private and the public sector. Loyalty has indeed grown to be the "ethical word of the time" in working life. But can it be? Loyalty can of course not be ethical before the core question is asked: "Loyalty towards what?" Without a certain degree of loyalty it is obvious that any organised practice is impossible, but without independent critical reflection on what is to be counted as acceptable practice, the loyalty is blind and by that uncritical. Organising, understood as institutionalised loyalty and strict chains of command, is not compatible with the fact that each individual is forced to live and work in a complex ethical reality. If we force responsibility into boxes, equalise responsibility with economic balance and expect loyalty to management-defined values and visions, we will be unable to identify what is ethically challenging and to exercise good judgement.

An understanding of ethics as following rules of a game without questioning what is a praiseworthy game – what constitutes an ethically good social practice – will always be insufficient. Rules of the game are closely attached to what one in philosophical terminology refers to as constitutive rules. These are rules that, in an economic context, are supposed to prevent cheating, fraud, assault against employees and contractual partners and bribery. In short, all conditions that may undermine the system and create other games if they are allowed to spread. An obvious example of such a violation of the rules is the growing number of cases we have seen in Norway recently of real estate agents using their position to their own advantage by doing business on their own behalf in the real estate market. Exploiting inside information (in economic terms, asymmetric information) for their own benefit will over the course of time demolish the trust the real estate agents, as marshals between seller and buyer, are heavily dependent upon in this market. They have a role that this indeed complex market depends on in order to function decently as an open market.

Such rules preserve the nature of the game, as we normally know it, and by that they preserve the efficiency of the market. But ethics is always more; ethics deals with values, basic considerations of the balance between different ways of creating meaning, and whether our appetite for life and important life content is won or lost. Social responsibility is not about how each company, as we often hear in the new speech of business life, sees itself served by taking care of the whole human being. It is rather about how each human being in striving for autonomous living finds itself caring for itself as a whole, and that this means caring about society as a whole – and by that, responsibility has to be understood as rationally based on a diversity of values and ways of organising.

It is in the elucidation of this intuitive basic point of ethics that we have to understand the social commission of the company – the social commission as it implicitly is given to a company, and how it continuously has to be renegotiated within economic practice. Business ethics includes both supporting the best possible management of this commission, that is, providing for a resource-efficient production and trade, and to challenge it by seeing its limits, to debate the framework of values given within the commission. This includes being critical to the idea of growth that is built into the operation of the system. Still, when ethics is demanded it is usually a breach of the internal rules of the game that is the triggering factor. And that this often is taken to be the most important approach. Let us here look at one example.

As part of the globalisation of economies, corporate social responsibility is often part of an important safeguard against exploitation of employees in developing countries. The case of sweatshops is a recurring phenomenon in business ethics textbooks. It has for instance been revealed that inside the fast-growing Chinese economy a large number of bidders for industrial production hide infringements of basic health and security standards from their investors.

This is of course worrying, and if globalisation is to result in a humane working life in more parts of the world, development of responsibility on the level of the single economic actor is a key factor. Without such responsibility it is difficult to imagine that poor working conditions can not be used as a competitive advantage in global competition. But the ethical problems do not stop here. Rather it is here they start – at least start getting more demanding. The Chinese production of cheap consumer goods is one of the main conditions that have made it possible for the western – and parts of the non-western – middle class of the world to increase their consumption considerably the last 5 to 10 years. And ethically, we have to ask what good this actually causes, what kind of welfare it raises, whether it does cause substantial growth in demand for goods that really matter in peoples lives when viewed in relation to other critical conditions, such as the energy and environmental disadvantages that it contributes to.

## Social responsibility as a media phenomenon

Social responsibility is however usually awakened as a media phenomenon when something obviously has gone wrong *within* and not *with* the market – when weak, single parties are unfairly treated, when greed grows too big or when innocent third parties are directly hurt or threatened by the activities of a company. Or if the market distributes goods in a way that is so obviously unreasonable that some people start wondering who has seized unauthorized power. In other words: social responsibility is demanded when one immediately understands that something has gone wrong but does not need to challenge the institutional framework within which it has gone wrong.

This of course is connected to the fact that discussions of social responsibility often operate with a concept of responsibility that does not shape our vision of companies but one that points towards companies as shaped by the social commission given to them. And by that it is defined and anchored within the value-based frames of business life. There has been a lot of discussion about how bad attitudes of managers and employees lead to wrong action and how economic decision-making may influence the society around the company negatively. With that we often see focus placed on what goes wrong, like a toxic spill, challenging downsizing or scandals of corruption, or instances when we all as consumers are cheated. When the extraordinary happens – what is not supposed to happen, but is still rather easily recognised – more social responsibility is quickly called for.

It is clearly both illegal and morally wrong for shops to operate with discounts based on fictive prices; it is misleading for us as customers, much the same as when chain stores give price guarantees on products that can only be found in their own shops. But even if this is a substantial breach of moral codex, the internal rules of the game that have to apply in decent business life, it is not here we find the most substantially challenging, ethically speaking, in the economy. More important than decency within given frames is where and how the frames are shaped and where they are placed. To protect us as customers against rude market power is of course important, also with respect to business ethics, but it is not always the most important aspect in the debate on social responsibility. In this debate it is more important to draw the lines and define when we should think and act as consumers – and when we, for the sake of sustaining other kinds of goods, primarily need to fill other roles.

We can say that the visible demand for social responsibility in a media society is greatest when the need for conscientiousness, as I see it, is least, and least when the need actually is greatest. It is when action floats casually that the critical thinking fades, and this is when the dominant understanding of economy asserts its grip over our minds. Without a deeper critique of the system, much of the talk about corporate social responsibility ends up as hegemonic thinking, casting a veil of linguistic fog over our discussions, or ends at best as a somewhat Aristotelian debate on the deeds of managers. When one is asked to stick to the point, that is, to think within the given frames of economic practice, one usually ends up making obvious and rather plain indications of the worst greed, etc.

Social responsibility should apply to the language and the models of thinking that we more or less unconsciously accept as natural tools for understanding ourselves, guiding our choices and shaping our ideas of freedom. Challenging the one that feels free, simply by the model of the consumer's freedom to choose, does not have to be a result of invidious paternalism, but can be seen as part of an important process, realising how your thinking and ways of action are often based on presumptions you yourself are unaware of. Accordingly, the assumption is that we have to obtain transparency in the power structure both inside and around ourselves. Obtaining this can obviously start with asking "how much is *enough for me*, and when will more (in terms of material goods and status-seeking) ruin my ability to enjoy what I have and my non-economic values?" No agreed-upon working life ethics can replace questions that deal with what we live for, how work, money and consumption are connected to experiencing richness of meaning, vitality and good feeling in everyday life.

This is why it is so important that an analysis of economic power focus on all the small events that create the general picture of everyday life. Any large picture is created from many so-called small events. All the small pieces of tastefulness and fun in the fascinating world of new products, all the minor cutting of costs, all the extensions of advertising area, all the small steps toward further privatisation – of which each and every one seem safe, often as natural steps of modernization and development. Is it really such a big problem that teddy-bear-like chocolate products from the Norwegian chocolate producer Nidar dwell in their own world in cyber-space targeting children? Or can it be wrong that fire engines are covered in advertisements? Or that the watch producer Citizen launches a slogan saying that the watch is what shows who you really are? Or that public services such as snow removal and transport of prisoners are put on public tender? Or that some Norwegian communities are allowed to supplement their poor finances by accepting advertising on their (often frequently visited) home pages, or put advertising screens in the corridors of the city hall?

Once having started asking these questions, and particularly within the framework of economic logics, it becomes difficult to define the limit for "when it gets to be ethically problematical". Many Norwegian football stadiums have been given commercial names recently – so why not auction the name of the railway station or the main street of the city to the highest bidder? The fact is that there are no real answers to these "small" questions unless we move out of the dominant market economic logic and ask the ethical questions of which non-economic goods we value in and of themselves, in an intrinsic rather than an instrumental manner.

## The freedom – and surrealism – of the consumer society

The "logofication" of the visible infrastructure of society will of course lead our ethical attention in the direction of the basis of economy – consumption. Advertising and branding have like any other business activity their bases in needs and social processes among consumers. Nevertheless, consumer ethics is such a large theme that it can not be fully addressed here. We will only try to visualise some of the feelings of alienation that can be said to be among the core elements of consumer ethics and by that show why the concept of social responsibility is not singly attached to the producers' side of an economy but also needs to be incorporated in the role of the consumer.

The alienation we will discuss here is not the result of brutal use of power by some identified external part, or of insulting deprival of freedom. It is rather, paradoxically at least on the surface of it, a celebration of freedom, a celebration that slowly but definitely slips into a paradoxical state, consisting of a mix of apathy and hyperactivity. Consumer freedom is per definition negative freedom in liberal terms; actually it is often *the* model of freedom where the core is to act without external limitations. It is a freedom that we welcome but that we just a bit too late realise is also a source of frustration and social insecurity – and with that a deprival of elements of our diverse, positive freedom. In other words, it is not solely an archetypal freedom but also a *typical* freedom where we too easily fall into the patterns of culture, weakening our independent thinking. In sharp and "unscientific" terms: once the mild but stubborn curtain of habit is drawn aside we see the almost unlimited madness of consumer culture. We see the bizarre fascination of everything new, the hilarious styling of body and clothes, a deeply sad fear of not being able to appear in an acceptable manner that keeps us frenetically occupied with our image creation, the resource-destructive *need* to replace furniture and decoration, the sad joy over the new SUVs and flat screens, and we see the absurd neuroses of interior design ("the kitchen of this spring...!") – it is all a surreal mix of blind technologic optimism, calculated seduction, weakened autonomy and lacking foothold.

We get to see that which we normally do not see, namely, all the matters that lead to a scary conformity and a monotonous everyday life that slowly is emptied of meaning. We see that things create distance rather than lasting satisfaction – distance between people and also between ourselves and the vivid life we want to live. The point and the problem is of course that we are talking about a rather comfortable condition of alienation. Usually it will appear as a grumbling, a mild discomfort, a discomfort that – again rather a paradox – it feels adequate to try to shop our way away from. If we put it into a larger perspective we will see that much of the growing consumption in the western world and the increasingly more dominating consumer-lifestyle (the "consumerism") appear as thoughtless consumer hysteria rather than an increase in welfare. Some may state that it even assumes an aggravating lack of perspectives, as here:

> We "over-consumers" can not see the connection between our lives and the ecological systems and processes that actually carry our existence. We live in the cities, doped by the systems and other technology, far away from the slums of Bombay, from the underpaid workers of China and from the copper mines in Zambia. We are alienated, physically and psychically from the enormous pressure that our way of living exerts on the rest of the planet. And what we can not see we do not fear.[17]

But we do not really need to see it this way, connected to the obviously challenging problems in our natural environment, to see the point about consumer alienation. We can stick to what concerns our social life and our own quality of life. In an article with the rather suggestive title, "Are We Worthy of Our Kitchens?" Christine Rosen asks what kind of homes – and society – we create around our technology and material goods. We can not run away from the fact that this is all very much a question of status, about the dream of growing respect and of the fear of not being good enough. And the actual

---

[17] From "Dyster utvikling i økosystemet", an article by Wayne Ellwood, in the newspaper *Friheten*, which can be found at http://www.friheten.no/lang/2000/11/wayne.html. My translation from Norwegian.

possibility of achieving what we want seems to be further and further away as we get trapped into a web of continously renewed order of social distinctions in the marketplace.

Hunting for status is actually not about money and what it can provide in terms of material goods. It is about being able to stand up as something special, about attention and respect. And understood in this way, consumption is close to a zero-sum-game, and we touch on an understanding of why the quest for social status will not decrease as material wealth grows, or as the Norwegian monitoring company MMI ever so often finds in its examination of Norwegian values (Norsk Monitor): the feeling of happiness seems to be completely independent of how much we own. And as Rosen points out: many people justify buying the latest household machines as a way of saving time, but family life seem as rushed as ever. Judging by how Americans spend their money – on shelter magazines and kitchen gadgets and home furnishing – domesticity appears in robust health. Judging by the way Americans actually live, however, domesticity is in precipitous decline [18] It is surely not only Americans whose household income is of a size that affords the possibility to buy a lot of the things that matter, but where business and restlessness deprive them of the possibility to put these things into the right, cherished social contexts. The products stand apart from the good life they are supposed to support. The only impact they have is as a display of successfulness. What else can this be than an everyday surrealism – and lack of responsibility?

From these examples of consumer criticism that do not address the obviously problematic aspects of the environment and the global allocation of welfare, we can look at some elements that deal with our social emotions and which in fact seem to contradict this conclu-

---

[18] An article in *The New Atlantis – A Journal of Technology and Society*, winter 2006. It can be found at http://www.thenewatlantis.com/archive/11/rosenprint.htm.

sion. Emotions focused on things are often deemed bad or less-worthy, like facsimilies of genuine intimacy and love between people. Consumers shopping for goods that offer emotional linking are often assessed as doing so-called compensatory consumption. The fascination and love for things is therefore often assessed as misguided social emotions. And misguided emotions usually lead to disappointment and a feeling of emptiness, and the result is often a callous and indifferent consumer. To put it sharply: consumption leads to empty and sometimes rather painful posing.

But, on the other hand, we can claim that consumption is not a sole, limited practice where happiness automatically means getting hold of more goods. Consumption is involved in most of our social relations, and it can be said to be an integral part of our ways of creating meaning. This stretches from the simple act of looking for attention and acknowledgement in the eyes of people you meet on the street, to the more complex symbolic interchange that creates the complete life of a family – things that we would hardly claim unethical. Consumption can of course hide a lot of unhappy escape from reality. One can try to mend lost love by shopping and entertainment. Lack of friendship can be covered behind the latest in fashion. Hobbies, collecting and games can be obsessive and those truly, passionately occupied by interior design must be said to have locked their feelings into both a narrow and shallow field of possibilities.

But at the same time it has to be said that aspects of such a consumer critique rely on a rather dubious social ideal of direct and pure contact between humans. This is a romantic conception of direct connections between people unmediated by goods and services – a conception that establishes itself in this comment expressed by Thor Øivind Jensen: "It has actually come to be a hallmark of humanistic quality not to care about things"[19]. The core of the argument to

---

[19] Jensen (2005, p. 231). My translation from Norwegian.

which this expression belongs, an argument that represents a so-called political view of consumption, is that for each human the feeling of being oneself and owning one's life has to have real substance, a materialized content, and that this content very well can include different consumer actions and emotions directed toward things.

Still, there are a large number of examinations like the one mentioned above, which conclude that more consumption does not necessarily give rise to more happiness. Though one must say there is something rather peculiar about this idea in the first place, that there actually *should be* any direct relationship between consumption and feelings of happiness. Is it not the case that the reported feeling of happiness, despite what can supposedly be expressed in such empirical surveys, is actually woven into a rather complex web of mental and social factors? One can of course claim – faithful to the basic ideas of postmodernism – that postmodern society is disconnected from any welfare-based legitimacy of production, that legitimacy is found in some completely different kind of phenomena; simply in the wide range of innovative, spectacular and image-creating activities. That science and technology and the commercial exploitation of same are united in a spectacular economy of role-play, change and self-creation, closely connected to such cultural elements as the shocking effects of art, the exhibitions of the entertainment industry and the aesthetic and extreme achievements of sports.

Even if such an analysis definitely provides understanding of important sides of consumer society that have not been visualised in traditional economic analyses, a critical analysis of private consumption has to take into consideration values, perspectives and long-term assessments that are not necessarily visible to the consumers themselves. Some sort of ideology criticism is ethically necessary. A complete psychological analysis of consumption – or a corresponding symbolic analysis of culture – will always be in danger of trivialising and partly obscuring the ethical sides of consumption. A long term perspective of one's own consumption is something that one has to *fight for*, given that it is cognitively, emotionally and practically demanding.

We need of course to separate between ethically dubious materialism (being mentally caught by and attached to things) and a life that includes material goods as carriers of symbolic value and that provide a rich and meaningful life. Nevertheless a steadily growing consumption is fuel for ethical discussion. If we are to bring these considerations down to earth for discussion, it is, again, all a matter of what our perspectives make visible and by that possible for us to consider. The role of the consumer will in many ways invite a measure of blindness from responsibility. In this role it is easy to view discount airline tickets as a good. We do not see that air traffic is one of the largest contributors to climate gas pollution, and that the pollution created by two persons travelling by plane from Oslo to Spain and back is the same as what a family car emits over the course of a year. And when the possibility of environmental taxes related to air traffic arises, consumers react negatively, which again leads to low-price airlines threatening to move their routes to neighbouring countries. Economic growth seems to be fed by an obstinate and mutually intensive spiral of repudiation of responsibility between economic actors.

## The itching question

No matter which scientific perspective we employ to understand the mechanisms of consumption, and by that, understand economic growth, there arises the inescapable question, "Why growth?" "Why even more?" In this connection, when the question is how can we best understand social responsibility, we need to ask: is it only because of the internal necessity of the system – an economic system that demands a real personal effort to break out and say that it is enough, and that considers it a peculiarity if one invests in something that does not increase the monetary value of one's assets, and that, at bottom, perceives it as a threat against society if too many are willing to settle for the level of material welfare they have already achieved. Transferred to the production side of economy we experience what Fredrik Engelstad points out in the book *Hva er makt (What Is Power)*: the demand for profitable operation and more efficiency are in principle insatiable – profit can never be high enough.[20]

When money stacks at some level of society – as it may in many rich, oil-producing countries like Norway – but also in private hands, this will of course bring up importunate questions regarding values. Stein Erik Hagen – one of the richest men in Norway – is an archetypical self-made man who built his fortune in grocery stores, sold out and was left with a multi-billion kroner fortune. As the Norwegian journalist Gudleif Forr notes: "This is classical capitalism. But what has he done to move on? What has he created? Has he transferred his talents to other parts of the society and given Norway growth and progression? Stein Erik Hagen has put his money in the Orkla corporation, but he has not yet given any signals of restructuring – except for selling Orkla Media, a disorderly process that now is in danger of ending as a complete fiasco. And if it is successful it will not lead to anything – except for more money, for him included".[21] We see something that may have come to be the norm – where it is absurd to demand that large amounts of money can be used for the development of society that does not include profit. Big money is supposed to result in even more money, anything else seems quite simply to be unreasonable, and even perceived by many to be irresponsible.

The Norwegian philosopher Jon Hellesnes reminds us that this is a theme that has been discussed in much of the classical modern literature concerning human alienation:

---

[20] Engelstad (2005). My translation from Norwegian.
[21] From the article "Bursdag på Rimi" in *Dagbladet* 21th July 2006. My translation from Norwegian.

Martin Heidegger had a good point when he, in several so-called late writings, indicated: "Das gestell", that is, technological and economic-administrative systems, are given a substantial power, in particular when it has no goal beyond itself, when their own reproduction and expansion is the only existing goal.[22]

We have to ask if we now are clever enough in challenging this power. And if we are not, we have to ask whether, due to some shortcoming of our formal education we lack a wide enough critical basis for discussing economic questions. Without building too much heroism into this, we can at least say that looking for social responsibility is to search for the heretical questions. The questions not easily accepted within our dominant sphere of thought. As I write this there are 41 Porsche Cayenne automobiles announced for sale on the Norwegian website finn.no, ranging in price from 900 000 NOK to 2 200 000 NOK (approximately 110 000 to 275 000 Euro). There is no reason to believe that there will be fewer during the next year. (Besides this car is now so "common" that it in some circles is considered rather cheapish – it does not function as an effective social distinction anymore.) In relatively nouveau rich Norway we experience a tremendous expansion in the direction of searching for status, a status that almost as a law of nature can be interpreted as materialistic and realised in consumption. Can social responsibility, we may ask, be confined to the decency of the companies that produce this type of car?

---

[22] Hellesnes (2004, p. 113). My translation from Norwegian.

Chapter 2

# Companies and social responsibility

A pragmatic perspective

Can a corporation announce its social responsibility at the same time that it shuts down or dramatically reduces the activity in profitable companies? And is it at all possible to talk about responsibility for society without discussing what kind of society is actually desired?

## More than economy?

The much-discussed "Union-case" in Norway (where the Norwegian wood-processing company Norske Skog, during autumn 2005 decided to shut down its activity in the city of Skien) clearly shows the tension between profit and ethics and makes it urgent to discuss this popular, but rather indistinct concept of responsibility. And this is a difficult notion to discuss, partly because discussing it is (de)constructing it. Corporate social responsibility is from time to time written off as out of date – as part of a distant past with an actual concept of collective citizenship – while it in other cases is profoundly defended in business life itself as an important element in visualising the value creation of commercial business. As a third path academics in different disciplines try to redefine the concept and give it new content by extending the bottom line to also include the effects on the natural environment and respect for human rights, or by regarding the company itself as a (local) society with responsibility for the whole human being[23].

In this chapter I will present quite a radical understanding of corporate responsibility by giving it status as a value-critical concept that finds its basis in the root of our economic ideas, and demonstrating this by challenging the concept of work itself. Critical thinking includes feeling that the framework of thinking is too rigid. One of the most difficult aspects of practical criticism is attempting to step away from the basic antagonisms of our time, such as the idea of a fundamental difference between ethics and profit. Even if one believes that behaving "ethically correct" will be profitable in the long run – as the well-known mantra of "doing well by doing good" indicates – or if one feels that what is really ethical has to be done independently of what is profitable (doing right for right's own sake), the thinking will be based on a division between the good or right (the ethical) and the profitable (the economical).

Social responsibility is not a concept that concerns the internal affairs of a company or the relationship between the company and its surroundings as regulated in a given economic context. Social responsibility must, as described in chapter one, reside in challenging power – economic power both in a material and a symbolic sense.[24] A cardinal part of this power consists of splitting economic interest and ethics into two different spheres of human life, so that economic life can develop in line with "its own laws" – and ethics can be introduced as a "limiting or possibly profitable factor". With this understanding as a background, a headline on Nordic companies in the global mar-

---

[23] This last approach is advocated by, among others, the American philosopher Robert C. Solomon. See Solomon (1997) for a brief introduction to his well-known Aristotelian position in business ethics.

[24] Meyer (2003, p. 18–19). My translation from Norwegian.

ket in the Norwegian newspaper *Dagens Næringsliv*, in an annex focusing on CSR, actually could be: "Full of Ethical Competitiveness". Here we see Nordic egalitarianism translated into competitive advantages in the market. In short, a way of thinking that contrasts my own.

Siri Meyer has presented a clarification of symbolic power and its consequences that suits my purpose here: "The power to create and maintain a collective area of understanding and action and to establish and maintain differences can be called symbolic power. Symbols create reality; they give the world meaning, values and impact, and they define limits… Language and images recognised as true descriptions of reality are ascribed major power… Symbolic power will usually be invisible. The recognition of the symbolic power often occurs unconsciously."[25] Coupled with such a wide concept of power is a radical interpretation of responsibility that implies that companies can not themselves define the range of their social responsibility. A real criticism of the values in our economic practice has to take the form of dialogue between responsible human beings not being tied by loyalty to a company community – or more fundamentally, without having their thoughts swayed by the language and the images of economic values, choice and distribution of today's dominant goods. I will basically anchor this radical interpretation in new pragmatic philosophy. The girder in such an understanding is the importance of open dialogue and public debate of values, something I will return to more explicitly at the end of this chapter.

Both CSR and CC (corporate citizenship) are new, central words in this debate. They can both be translated as referring to the social responsibility of the company. And as we find written in a current book on social responsibility and corporate citizenship in the light of the UN's Global Compact: "This means that the honesty and integrity of directors is as much up for discussion as waste packaging

---

[25] Meyer (2003, p. 18-19). My translation from Norwegian.

and child labour ... These corporations are *our* corporations; they are our heart and soul. In them we invest our pensions, our working lives and our customs. When they act, they act as both private and public entities."[26] Through the concept of social responsibility it is acknowledged that companies should conceive of their decision horizon in a wider sense than just creating more profit for the stock owners. The argument is that companies participate in shaping our values and society as a whole. Understood in this way, it can truly be expressed by saying that it is all about much more than economy. Though what we call pragmatism in philosophy will have a sceptical approach to any construction of absolute lines of demarcation, whether the lines are between reason and sensibility, body and soul, theory and practice or between consciousness and "the world itself". Thus any division between our earthly interests and needs, on the one hand, and a higher and purer form of reason on the other will also be challenged. Accordingly, in this philosophical line of thought there is no ahistorical, contextless division between ethics and economy, or duty and self-interest.

Reasonable interpretations of ethics as "more than economy" have to imply that economic responsibility is anchored in a more basic ethical concept of responsibility, and that profit does not automatically represent desirable value creation. We need therefore to ask if the task of business ethics has to be to find a *way out of* such a fundamental division and not to analyse its way down into it. It is a rather trivial acknowledgement that ethical responsibility is more than economic calculations. It is, to put it simply, more about being able to reflectively endorse goals than about the pure calculation of means. But the concept of social responsibility means that we are not acting reflectively only towards the goals of the company; we must also take into account the goals of society. And then the perspective

---

[26] McIntosh/Thomas/Leipziger/Coleman (2003, p. xi).

opens up and ethical and economic considerations have to be thought of as fused together in human action.

Debating the relationship between ethics and profit, then, is obviously more than economy, in the sense that some of the value premises have to be found in other spheres than the economic sphere. But if we understand it as Aristotle did, as wise house-keeping integrated into the practice of social life, it is not necessarily *something else than* or *apart from* economy. Then we see economy correctly understood in human life as a whole[27]. It is in the extension of this that philosophical pragmatism offers some good insights.

## The concept of responsibility in pragmatic ethics

Erik Lundestad approaches social responsibility along these lines:[28] based on classical American pragmatism (John Dewey in particular) he argues that in professional work with social responsibility we do not need to justify any joining together of economy and ethics. We should rather show how ethics and economy in practice will always be connected and that profit in economic terms is always ascribed meaning in relation to non-economic values. It is my opinion, though, that Lundestad pays too little attention to how this will be if we extend the perspective and see social responsibility not only based on a company's need for profit but also consider the company as an integral part of a democratic, liberal society. Then other and more basic value problems arise. Therefore I want to supplement more than challenge his approach. But first we need to discuss which theoretical insights and which concept of responsibility result from this pragmatic thinking.

---

[27] See my book, Nyeng (2002, particularly the introduction and chapter I) for a brief description.
[28] Lundestad (2005).

Corporate social responsibility is an ethical concept and consequently has to be attached to a deeper understand of ethics. In business ethics we find three dominating lines of thought: utilitarian, Kantian and Aristotelian ethics. They are principally different regarding criteria of moral rightness and goodness, but share the understanding that it is possible to anchor and justify morality philosophically, in some basic theoretical view of calculating welfare, universal duties and a particular view of human happiness, respectively. In pragmatic philosophy though, one denies that there exist any philosophical insights that can contribute to ethical problem solving. Even if philosophy offers clarification of concepts and descriptions that can stimulate thinking, we can find no philosophical support for our basic interpretations of values. There are no valid first principles independent of time, place and human self-understanding.

One of the most central philosophers here is the much-debated American pragmatist Richard Rorty. And Rorty's liberal imperative – which he summarizes in the slogan "don't be cruel" – has normative power, not by reflecting a philosophical truth, but by tying us to a tradition where protecting others from cruelty has the highest value. As Rorty expresses in an interview: "But Plato was wrong. There are no first principles. You look around, you read history, and you end up sensing what is important and what is not. Then you declare something, for example that evil actions are the worst we can do. It is only a slogan summarizing your reaction to what you read or experience."[29] If concrete stories about human cruelty can not get people to share our opinion on this subject, ethical theory can not do the job either. His pragmatic understanding of ethics is contextual but at the same time comprehensive. And the core element of the content in this ethics is the respect for value pluralism and for the

---

[29] Richard Rorty in an interview in the Norwegian newspaper *Morgenbladet*, October 7, 2005, with the headline, "Pragmatic Social Democrat".

growth and development of the human being. It is a deeply liberal core in the new pragmatic ethics, but this liberality has little in common with the focus on rights in a juridical sense that characterizes philosophical liberalism in the Kantian casting. This gives important implications for the relationship between theory and practice and therefore for the perception of responsibility.

Questions such as "How do you decide when to fight for social justice, and when can you indulge in private activities?", "Is it justifiable to sacrifice two innocent people in order to save four others?" and "When can you favour your own (friends or family) in preference to complete strangers?" have no principal answers. Anyone who believes it possible to find theoretical answers to such questions lives in a metaphysical delusion. All we can do is to listen to different stories – from a multitude of sources in literature, media, art, philosophy, everyday life – and arrive at our own opinions within our horizon of values and the language we use. Our models for moral behavior are the practical conventions, the anecdotes and the stories, and our ethical orientation will develop from concrete stories about greed, fraud and assault. The connection to more abstract philosophical concepts will arise subsequently, based on our experiences. Here it is natural to refer to Aristotle who pointed out that claiming a reason for everything will expose both bad manners and lack of understanding.

So what will such an understanding of ethics imply? A point with major impact is that it is not possible to abandon or be disloyal to a community that one does not feel a belonging to or see oneself as a member of. The ethical dimension actually resides in identification with a belonging to a larger community. Morally we understand ourselves based on our connections and our relations. Ethical responsibility consists in acknowledging that the responsibility actually rests on us, here and now, and can not be handed over to anybody else without us failing. The question of social responsibility that follows from Rorty's pragmatic concept of solidarity is without references to universal human rights or ahistorical forms of rationality.

The question becomes: what does solidarity with our society involve? This liberal democracy that I live in – how can it best be defended and improved? How can we take care of it so that no one will systematically suffer under their autonomous choices in life? Ethical values are consequently values that arise when we appeal to a "we" and an "us", to intentions that mirror attitudes in a community that we feel we genuinely belong to (so-called "we-intentions"). Worth mentioning here is that ethical dilemmas accordingly will arise from the fact that our identity will be connected to several communities that we do not want to fail. According to pragmatic philosophy, therefore, ethical dilemmas are neither rare nor extraordinary in our everyday practice (nor can they be solved according to a theory).

There is of course a historical element included here that will explain Rorty's limited belief in philosophical theory. According to Rorty the time of theories is gone, we have all the theoretical accounts of human responsibility we need; the problem is no longer philosophical, but practical. It concerns motivation and implementation of shared values. It is about the motivation for fighting severe social injustice, discrimination, poverty and the lack of legal rights protecting the individual, and the implementation of liberal institutions that can administer, as already stated by John Stuart Mill, the right balance between protection of privacy and preventing evil and suffering. But even with such a different understanding of the sources of ethics, we do not speak of a less strict concept of responsibility. It is rather the contrary: if an economic system contributes to isolation and the creation of humiliating conditions for particular groups, and in addition demolishes the desire and ability of people to enjoy their existence, it will be a system we, if we take our social responsibility and our identity seriously, need to criticise.

The concept of responsibility that we are discussing here is postmodern in the sense that it is disconnected from paramount stories or so-called grand narratives (ideologies) about social development. The human being possesses dignity, not by realising a plan included in its nature, but by actively supporting – and being willing to fight for – concrete aspects of society and its traditions. The core element in Rorty's pragmatism is therefore an urge to concretely defend the liberal, democratic society and its universal welfare system. In this we see a consciousness of the historical allocations with a strict demand for action. And we see the fragile and vulnerable in our own equality-oriented civilisation. An acknowledgement that the growth of liberal democracies in the western world is a historical contingency and not a logical development along a given axis of human rationality. There is, as Berntstein states: "no historical necessity, no destiny, no enduring human essence that ensures that the freedom of democratic, liberal society will prevail." [30] And this vitalises our own status as moral actors and by that, as mentioned, the need to focus on an economic system that threatens the diversity of values in society and that can be said to make differences in class and status limit the lives of steadily growing parts of the population.

Therefore, as a prolongation of this, it is necessary to state that companies *do* have an extended social responsibility – something that is not given, but as a point of view has to be contended – in order to get closer to *what* this responsibility actually concerns. The answer to this is highly dependent on whether we see responsibility as an addition to an economic profit goal, or if we have as our basis that business life and economic rationality take part in the overall shaping of our value judgments and our ideas of a desirable development of society. It is hard for me to see how it can be possible to pragmatically claim that the latter, system-critical approach should not take precedence in a discourse on responsibility. The goal can not funda-

---

[30] Bernstein (2003, p. 134).

mentally be to shelter an ethically improved growth of economic values, but has to be to challenge the framework underlying ideas of such growth.

My interpretation of new pragmatic philosophy will therefore result in the view that it seems too easy to step aside from the critique of the system in business ethics, by for instance making it all a matter of personal courage, dignity and honesty in business life. In this way the criticism of the system escapes into a blind zone of virtue ethics, where focus is primarily put on the manager's ability to step up and, in the effort for economic profit, be led by her ethical qualities. In such an escape we of course see a fear of getting political – but a political view of economy is inevitable. As long as economic thinking and activity, more than ever, seem to set the premises, not only for development of the material aspects of our civilisation and our ecological prospects, but also for the dominant attitudes toward life and personal growth, the debate on values in society has to be a part of business ethics. The basic question related to corporate social responsibility is exactly – *responsibility for what?* With what should we feel solidarity; for what should we take responsibility?

## Social responsibility – for what?

Nevertheless, the ways companies manage responsibility often coincide with the popular and – from an ethical point of view, often empty – pursuit of company identity. A pursuit often seen as and expressed by positive and turgid formulations of values like "credibility", "accountability", "team spirit", "content customers", "cooperation", "involvement", "integrity" and "professionalism", which are often expressed with substantial power and enthusiasm within the work establishing a company culture. Rolf Lunheim is one of those who, rather subacidly, points out this often unrealistic infatuation with visions and values: "Many modern corporations seem to exceed new religious movements in digging into their soul and in the preaching of values."[31] Others, like Lars Klemsdal of the Norwegian Work Research Institute, refer to it as hysteria of visions that may threaten organizational culture and that offends the employee's rights.[32]

In addition to the fact that such a management of CSR results in a discourse of goodness that is difficult if not impossible to question (how is it possible to not embrace things like team spirit and professionalism?), it is difficult to understand as anything else than a movement that reinforces an economy focused on growth. To put it sharply, one can say that it is hegemonic nonsense that does not challenge but rather amplifies the power of economy – strategic action with new means – lacking attachment to any deeper value questions that challenge the system and open our eyes to exactly what social responsibility is directed toward.

A first step in this direction can be exemplified by a statement made by John Orlando who, through a utilitarian argumentation, claims that large workforce reductions, where the only goal is achieving further profit (so-called downsizing), usually are unethical. It is an argumentation genuinely directed towards society which focuses on the ethically doubtful in harming one to benefit others, and on the problem of justice and the question of legitimate expectations. In addition, the way he connects negative outcomes from discharge to the ownership structure of companies is rather opportune: "But an act of downsizing that merely increases profits which seems increasingly the case, requires a careful analysis of the harms and benefits it will incur to the parties involved. For a small firm, such as a fast-food franchise with a single proprietor, the owner may be at greater risk than her employees… However, with a large corporation, the results

---

[31] Lunheim (2005, p. 101).
[32] See the Norwegian newspaper *Dagens Næringsliv*, 26th June 2006, under the headline "Visjonshysteri i næringslivet (Hysteria of Visions in Business)".

are likely to be quite different."[33] This last point is also underscored by Sumantra Ghoshal: "The truth is, of course, exactly the opposite. Most shareholders can sell their stocks far more easily than most employees can find another job. In every substantial sense, employees of a company carry more risks than do the shareholders."[34]

Still, such an argument does not get completely to the root of the basic problems here. It takes a static perspective regarding the actual social conditions – the negative economical and emotional consequences of loosing one's job given the economic system and the social climate. It does not ask: why is not having a paid job the same as being an outsider, and loosing one's job the same as loosing face in our society? Why is it encumbered with mental and social costs? Why is social recognition connected to such a degree to work and economic profit?

It should be evident that a genuinely ethical interpretation of social responsibility can not be limited to only including a list of – often rather obvious – values in the building of internal organizational culture. Social responsibility has an *ethical* appeal precisely because it breaks with questions of culture within the company – precisely because it can not be defined through charismatic and visionary (or value-based) management. Actually one can say that it is quite the contrary – in the sense that the requested value consciousness legitimately can be directed toward questioning the idea of work and company life as the main sources of social value creation. How? A serious critique of value and culture in our time has to challenge the cultural pressure directed toward maintaining good health, establishing a career, submitting to life-long learning, and, more commonly, contributing to the community by energetic paid work. But in what sense are the disabled, free artists, financial speculators, academic and

---

[33] Orlando (2003, p. 45).
[34] Ghoshal (2005, p. 80).

industrial workers "in the same boat" with respect to work? Such a question is radical in the sense that it challenges the roots of social responsibility – the idea of a large community kept together by the economic value creation in "our" companies.

## A life beyond paid work?

This makes us wonder what working implies and what value creation provides – and to whom? I have not come across any clearer, critical statement concerning this than what the Norwegian professor in psychology, Arnulf Kolstad, stated recently: "Maybe we should take a closer look at the 'work' they perform. Then we will see that many of those 'working' are more of a burden to the community than those who do not participate in the production of goods and services. That what they produce has such excess cost to the society that rather than being a positive contribution, it taps into the resources."[35] Such reflections are deep in the sense that they challenge the platform of the concept of work. For as Kolstad further states: "In a society that increasingly destroys the environment and nature, creates burn-out and work addiction and stimulates an insane consumption, it might be we have reached the time to relax and sleep a little more." The art of life can, as we know, consist of being engaged in small things in a substantial manner. Is this an artificial conclusion? It is at least nonetheless relevant in a debate concerning the content of social responsibility than the professional perspectives based on the unproblematic, prevailing comprehension of the concepts of work, profit and value creation.

Therefore the radical question has to be if freedom in our culture does not actually mean being free *from* paid employment and increas-

---

[35] Chronicle entitled "Ta det med ro (Take It Easy)", in the Norwegian newspaper *Dagbladet*, 24th January 2006.

ingly growing consumption – and the self-reinforcing spiral and less autonomous choices created by these powers. If we are to circumvent this and to suspend the business and ethical antagonisms between ethics (as demands/limitations) and profit (as a measure of an ethically neutral outcome of economic activities), a new thinking around the non-economic goals of economic activities understood as manufacturing practice has to be made. The way has to be found within a concept of "enough" – critical reflection over substantial values, pleasure and enjoyment. Without such reflection it is impossible to establish a basis for justification and limitation of the everlasting (measurable) growth. Truls Wyller, a Norwegian professor in philosophy, offers rudiments of such a social liberal criticism, not based in collective interests as something that rise above the interests of individuals, but with a basis in enlightened self-interest and enjoyment of life. It is here expressed in his criticism of capitalism pointing out the following paradox:

> This is a system that makes it a fact that even in wealthy countries working to obtain the means to enjoy life occupies so great a part of everyday life that for many people there is hardly room for actually enjoying life.[36]

The goal is never realized and the means seem often to be transformed into a goal of their own. And he proceeds, with reference to the practice oriented view of good life presented by Aristotle: "In a really alternative world work would be a means to a life beyond work." Here it is natural to mention, as Wyller also does, the possibility of an institutional system of democratically defined, guaranteed minimum income, a practical effort fully justifiable from an equality

---

[36] Wyller (2005, p. 223) This criticism comes as part of an assessment of the criticism of capitalism presented by Marsdal/Wold (2004).

oriented, liberal ideological perspective, as something that can partly "turn around" the self-reinforcing work logic of capitalism. With subsistence covered by a reasonable income granted by society, work will attract the citizens that at least to some degree will be free from the economic power in the system, and it is an institution that can be created in ways that make work lucrative from the first hour. At the same time, it can be argued that such a system is both a more humane and a more effective way of helping the poor than the rather demanding and sometimes degrading bureaucratic systems we have today.

But as Wyller also states: "Today a life beyond work is not a real alternative, and one 'gets' work only as long as one contributes to increased capital value at least as much as the competitors. Under such conditions the problem of *social security* is that it should never reach a level where people who can work, refrain from doing so – normatively, because it is perceived as unfair that people receive without contributing; economically, because it leads to less growth. However the point of a reasonable guaranteed income is to accept the possibility of a life without work." The same approach can be applied to a certain degree in discussing a somewhat less radical system such as the 6-hour working day – not with respect to how expensive it would be for companies, but to whether the increase in free time and non-economic realisation of values would be reasonable overall, in comparison to the decline in (increased) productivity that might also result. Drawing the limits of economic logic and introducing new standards of values can not, as we pointed out in Chapter I, be evaluated by their narrowly defined costs alone, as "expensive initiatives", since these measures of costs are what the limits have actually been drawn for.

Such concrete considerations can easily be connected to Lundestad's statement that economic values, pragmatically speaking, are encapsulated in the non-economic life of society. Such a critical challenging of the concept of work shows us certain possible results of the fact that economic evaluation can not stand alone. To use a division presented by Hans Skjervheim[37]: secondary ethics, that which concerns action towards a goal being effective, decent and accountable, presupposes primary ethics, our reflection over what forms of practice are goals in themselves. If liberal society is to be directed towards protection of what its members perceive as valuable, it simply can not in the long run be based on an economy that undermines the possibilities people have of realizing and enjoying these practices.

Another aspect of this problem is of course the unfortunate effects an increasingly demanding life in the service of work carries for each and every one of us. Not as an incidental result, but as internally connected to the prevailing ideas of freedom and self-realisation that extend from economy to life in general. Arne Johan Vetlesen, a Norwegian professor in philosophy, is one who expresses this with great clarity:

> Forms of suffering such as being burnt-out, being paralyzed, anxiety and depression can be viewed as unintended consequences of social conditions that are normally considered as contributing to something positive, the realisation of individual freedom. Key words for the conditions I refer to here are mobility, flexibility and the ability to change. *Re-adjustment* is the tune of today.[38]

The late modern dynamics of change and freedom in working life are far from being merely personally stimulating. In other words, instead of creative change, the mastering of one's own life and enrichment in this new, rapid culture of working life, Vetlesen sees readjustment, forced choices and exhaustion. A real distance exists

---

[37] A division that among other places can be found in the essay *Etikken og dagleglivet sin moral (Ethics and the Morals of Everyday Life)* (printed in Skjervheim, 1996)

[38] Vetlesen/Henriksen (2004, p. 148).

between expressed ideology of self-realisation (mentioned as one of "the lubricants of the new market liberalism"[39]) and the consequences generated by the system in the shape of downsizing and dubious environmental practice – all by-products of the demand for further efficiency. Besides, alternative ways of life for the individual who opts for a career in business become fewer and harder to choose, and as a consequence of the same new liberal organisation of society the collective safety nets become poorer. In this picture, absence from work is most of all seen as an individual phenomenon and analyses are made based on medical "failures in the human machinery" (or failures in the working moral of the individual), at the same time as the structural circumstances as possible causes are hardly communicated at all.

This is not about the abomination of the market powers, but about how they correctly understood – that is, seen from a wider, ethical perspective – can represent one form of liberal freedom of action. Such a freedom has to be anchored in symbolic resources where everyone is given the necessary qualifications to, as the Norwegian philosopher Arne Næss points out in his philosophy of life[40], set goals that do not stop being meaningful as soon as they have been reached. Any such critique of the system will of course run into the argument that the competitive power of the nation will be impaired if efficiency is not continuously increased. It is, nevertheless, philosophically unbearable to let such an argument, from an economic science with a much narrower normative mandate than we usually comprehend, overshadow the deeper arguments of values concerning what we live and feel responsible for. Making demands for justification of value standpoints is not a departure from liberal society; it is an absolute condition of it.

---

[39] See Marsdal/Wold (2004).
[40] Næss (1998, see in particular p. 60–62).

## Pluralism in values, freedom and criticism of the system

The Norwegian philosopher Jon Hellesnes gives us a concise picture of this rather "suppressed" situation, a picture that fits with the earlier mentioned Union-case and along the lines of Richard Rorty's uneasiness concerning the social justice both within and between our liberal societies:

> The basis for market solutions is that we have to arrange ourselves rationally related to what is already the reality, which is that the economic level is what determines everything... Those who benefit from the diffusion of this way of thinking are above all the trans-national capitalistic entrepreneurs. By referring to "economic laws" and the constraint represented by "globalisation" and "the world market", they can gain even larger space of action. They can threaten with what consequences will follow if they do not gain access to such a space. Then they will have to transfer even more of the employment to Asia. The levels of wages and taxes have to be reduced even further in Europe.[41]

This is what is referred to as the "race to the bottom" in global capitalism: (too) high standards, for environment or working conditions, are used as arguments when production is moved or new investments are made in other countries. By reifying economic laws and the market mechanism one conjures up an idea of the powerlessness of managers that is ethically speaking highly troublesome. Pleading that crucial decisions are taken under the influence of external forces actually means the dehumanization of business. It is false consciousness with considerable practical consequences.

---

[41] Hellesnes (2004, p. 142).

And as long as the new market liberal way of thinking prevails, and competition is seen as the natural principle for coordinating economic action, even across national borders, the space for ethical reflection on business will remain constricted. But a basic concept in pragmatic philosophy is that there are no fixed realities, economic or otherwise, that we as human beings have to follow. The race to the bottom does not follow an economic, rational pattern that we merely, at best, can hope to correct. The role of ethics is not limited to guiding or correcting behaviour in a given system; it still can and should challenge our way of thinking about these issues and the right and power of defining central concepts given to certain groups – in short, the ways of constructing economic reality and negotiating meaning between groups in society. Ethical responsibility is about avoiding partiality, poverty of concepts and instrumental fallacies in our practical thinking. And when liberality and individualism are understood as deregulated capitalism and principal scepticism towards community solutions, the central ethical challenges will be to limit greed, to develop care for the plight of employees in this time of globalisation and to prevent too large differences between rich and poor.

As human beings we have many roles and belong to different communities where symbolic power is manifested. A special feature of economic power is that it is directly connected to our conception of such basic things as our freedom, welfare and self-realisation. And the diversity of values is threatened when we experience that the market itself has become the supplier of premises for a so-called liberal moral criticism of traditions and social solutions – in short when behaviour in the market becomes *the* model of free choices, self-realisation and individualisation. The legacy Richard Rorty inherits from John Dewey places, on the other hand, value pluralism and a complex notion of individual development and autonomy in the centre of liberal thought. Something which can be said to have great affinity with the American philosopher Elisabeth Anderson's pronouncement: "Call a person autonomous if she governs herself by principles and valuations she reflectively endorses."[42] This is a pronouncement fueled by her pluralistic concept of personal freedom in liberal society, a concept with considerable impact for any notion of social responsibility:

> Call a person free if she has access to a wide range of significant options through which she can express her diverse valuations... Because people value different goods in different ways, their freedom requires the availability of a variety of social spheres that embody these different modes of valuation. Freedom thus requires *multiple sphere differentiation* — boundaries not just between the state and the market, but between these institutions and other domains of self-expression, such as family, friendship, clubs, professions, art, science, religion and charitable and ideal-based associations.[43]

Precisely this kind of value pluralism provides a clear understanding of the market as a manifestation of one mode (among several) for valuation. Anderson points out that our rationality has to be connected to attitudes, to the way we express different kinds of assessments of different forms of community, and not primarily to a contextless principle of utility maximization. Ethics has to do with the way we draw the boarders between the market and these other arenas of valuation. Because "to argue that the market has limits is to acknowledge that is also has its proper place in human life. A wide range of goods are properly regarded as pure commodities. Among these are the conveniences, luxuries, delights, gadgets, and services found in most stores."[44] The difficult ethical-political task, with direct relevance to a value-critical understanding of corporate social responsibility,

---

[42] Anderson (1993, p. 142).
[43] Anderson (1993, p. 141).
[44] Anderson (1993, p. 166–167).

resides in exploiting the considerable advantages that lie in utilising the solutions of the market while at the same time as not allowing the market, based purely on an efficiency-related argumentation, to eat its way into the various areas of public and social good, areas of life where the core of our responsibility is developed and enhanced.

## Social responsibility within the company

The collectivism that lies in the fact that companies are attributed the ability to act responsibly consists, as mentioned, often of a concept of community values and strong expectations of loyalty to this community. This can in itself carry immorality – we know very well the whistle-blower case that has its source just here. Nevertheless there are also deeper ethical questions connected to this idea of a company community. It supports the idea of man as the competent and "freely positioned", perpetually available worker – an idea that contributes to consolidating paid work as the *real* form of value creation.

However, focusing on common values, virtue and the life that takes place in competitive business environments also give us rich ethical material, in the shape of what new-Aristotelian ethics often refers to as internal goods[45]: for instance the experience of mastering a new and demanding job, of succeeding together with others, the experience of exiting rivalry in a new market, the pleasure of reaching the goals of the company and contributing to progress – and also the experience of loosing with dignity. These are all value elements that build people's identities. And they can all be viewed as integral parts of a compound practice – as a complex social game – where we at the same time draw a web of lines of responsibility. In this way we can also see that robust working communities, characterized by a

---

[45] A concept from the philosophy of the new Aristotelian, Alasdair MacIntyre (see MacIntyre 1985, particularly chapter 14). For a brief clarification, see my book, Nyeng (1999, Chapter 3 on virtue ethics).

broad spectrum of participation, mutual trust and openness, work as a buffer against the worst effects of bad moral inside a company.

The link between management style, company culture and responsible action is obvious. Based on the criticism of the growing individualisation raised by Vetlesen, it is possible to claim that this web of responsibility is about to come unsown, precisely because the economic aspects are not to a sufficient degree taken into consideration as a part of the non-economic values, but rather are pushed forward at their expense. This can be illustrated by a description Lunheim gave of the development in Shell during the 1990s:

> An almost "academic" culture of management based on sturdy know-how, loyalty and safe conditions of employment was challenged by continuous reorganising and increasing insecurity ... The core of loyal, experienced and well-informed professionals that were confident within their positions and dared speak out when things went bad, was pushed out or forced into silence.[46]

In this way the ongoing work done to secure the legal protection of whistle-blowers can be seen as a juridical initiative that obviously addresses the symptoms and not the source of the problem. Realistically speaking, seen from the inside of economic practice, that is, it is possible to say that we at best can talk about how companies manage their economic responsibility in an extended sense of that term, rather than talk directly about their social responsibility as it is understood here. The myth of business as an amoral, economic activity still lives, as described in a new textbook on business ethics: "The myth of amoral business represents not only the way many people in and out of the business world perceive business but also the way many would like to continue to perceive business. It is much easier to deal

---

[46] Lunheim (2005, p. 105).

with dollars and cents than to deal with value judgements."[47] Thus companies can, 36 years after Milton Friedman's credo that the only social responsibility of a company is to increase profit[48], attempt to manage their social responsibility as an indirect responsibility, by claiming that the most efficient way of taking care of welfare and liberal society is by taking care of their own bottom line. The social task of the company is, "after all", of a purely economic nature.

But seen from a pragmatic point of view this understanding is highly unreasonable. It presupposes that economic and non-economic aspects can be easily parted in the lives of humans who are supposed to carry the responsibility. In order to, at a later stage, indirectly fuse economy and ethical responsibility together, one has to undertake several intellectual efforts. But social responsibility can not be broken down to its constituent parts and then later cobbled together. This is a scientific model of management that badly represents people's practical judgement. Responsibility can not primarily be placed at the collective level of the company, but has to be coupled with a concept of integrity and human dignity; a value-based self-respect that includes the whole identity of each employee. Consequently it is not possible to start with economic valuations as a model of responsibility, since responsibility can not be adequately understood without awareness of our entire world of social hopes and visions – what expresses our strong evaluations.[49] Nor

---

[47] De George (2006, p. 6).
[48] Friedman (1970).
[49] The separation between strong/identity-building and weak evaluations is central in the works of the Canadian philosopher Charles Taylor. In short, strong evaluations are characterized by drawing qualitative lines between different alternatives of action, where this at the same time is an evaluation of the motivation behind the action (for instance something can be characterised as brave or kind). In strong evaluation something is given status as having higher value, as opposed to in weak evaluation (that indeed can be complex and require balancing based on one's judgement) where assessments are made purely based on one's wishes or "utility". Furthermore, the point is that through strong evaluations the identity can be shaped – they constitute the identity and are expressive. (See Taylor 1992, in particular Chapter 2, and for an introduction see my book, Nyeng 2000, particularly Chapters 1 and 6.)

can it, therefore, be placed with an isolated, single human being; it must be connected to the dialogical interaction between human beings in arenas where the access to different cultural and symbolic resources enables each and every one to see their working lives in a larger perspective.

If people understand themselves – and build economic theory and models of management – based on dichotomised division of the ethical and the economic, the result will be a line of inappropriate and veiling dilemmas. And if questions of valid economic values are not seen as part of a communicative and dynamic picture of human reason, bad thinking can easily lead to wrong action. One can even claim, as does the Norwegian philosopher Lars Svendsen[50], among others, that as long as the focus is put on company identity, core values and ethical regulations which are not coupled with critical attention towards the basic goals of economic activity and growth, business ethics is reduced to a kind of stupidity. In short, it can easily result in casual initiatives – such as the Norwegian public energy efficiency enterprise, Enova SF's campaign teaching children to teach their parents to switch off the lights when they leave a room, while at the same time mum and dad are sitting in the living room planning a second bathroom with a steam shower and heated floor. Instead of searching for the possibility of a basic conflict of values between the increasingly more energy demanding, materialistic ideal of life and the ecological recourse situation, one chooses initiatives that *limit the growth* (or more truly: the growth in growth). As Arne Næss states: "We discuss which forms of energy we should commit to if energy consumption keeps on growing towards the year 2020, but we rarely discuss whether we should concentrate on reducing the energy consumption per capita in our society."[51] This is exactly the kind of

---

[50] Svendsen (2001).
[51] Næss (1998, p. 94).

value evaluation that can not be handled *within* the company, but still is at the core of our social responsibility.

## Openness and dialogue
## – a communicative concept of responsibility

As Ims and Jakobsen have pointed out, Norske Skog's managing director Jan Oksum made an issue of the fact that the management did not change their argumentation throughout the whole, aforementioned Union process.[52] They pointed out that this, just as much as being a sign of strength and firmness, can be seen as a limited ability to share other's perspectives. And it is precisely the diversity of perspectives that is significant related to pragmatism, which does not operate with an absolute and perpetual concept of truth. I will account for this somewhat further in Chapter 5. The main point here is that our reality is shaped by the perspectives through which we view things, perspectives that *can* be useful in promoting human interest in all its diversity. Oksum's (and others') fixed argumentation does not allow for this diversity, but closes the room of action around a given economic logic.

What we seem to need is a concept of a *dialogue-based cooperation* between the parties in business life, open to the stimulation of art and culture and intellectual life, and having the potential to challenge self-sufficient economic evaluations. It is all about making economic assessments rest on reasoning in the intersection between economy, ecology, culture and existential choices, which again actually is the purpose of promoting the conditions of communicative rationality in our society. It is of course primarily from a position of discourse ethics – as we most clearly see it with Jürgen Habermas and Karl-

---

[52] Presented in an article in the Norwegian newspaper *Morgenbladet*, 7th October 2005, under the headline "Mer enn økonomi" (More Than Economy).

Otto Apel – that such an emphasis on communicative rationality as a basis for economic rationality can be found in the landscape of philosophy.[53] But it is important to notice the positive relationship that can be seen between Rorty and a rationalist like Habermas with his focus on dialogue and belief in our rationality of conversation. What Rorty objects to is Habermas' propensity towards universalising, to attempt to anchor the norms of rationality in something that exceeds society and context, not the actual communicative understanding of an open, liberal society itself.

Ingebrigtsen and Jakobsen conclude: "It is our opinion that this is a necessary condition in order to develop a functioning economy within the framework of a democratic and value pluralistic society."[54] Here we can utilize Rorty's view on moral evolution, which sees solidarity as something developed locally and thereafter grows both in extent and depth. There is of course nothing wrong with patriotism, building strong forms of identity and belonging, as long as it does not hinder, but rather leaves room for identification and sympathy outwards. Such identification is not necessarily a given; it is a result of dialogue and interaction where one allows one's own opinions to be challenged. It is my conviction that it is all about understanding that making economic choices has do be done with an eye to allowing people to be whole persons. Therefore the possibilities for open dialogue are crucial – because only those able to integrate their experiences in open, confident exchange of views with others, can increase their self-understanding and gain a perspective of themselves as responsible persons. We "find ourselves" when we hear what we ourselves have to say about what is valuable to us. It is in dialogical reflection that we establish connections between what we actually value and what we find really valuable.

---

[53] A good Norwegian introduction to the communicative theory of action presented by Habermas can be found in Eriksen/Weigård (1999).
[54] Jakobsen/Ingebrigtsen (2004, p. 151).

But can this in any way be said to be companies' responsibility? I would put it the other way around: since ethical responsibility must be constructed and negotiated in social practice, would it not be curious, pragmatically speaking, if companies were social units freed from questions concerning such responsibility by a given logic of economic thinking? Companies are attributed responsibility in and by the processes that make them capable of living in the long run, and it is hard to see how living in the long run can be achieved without giving sufficient consideration to the value diversity, individually and collectively, that supplies the economy with resources and gives meaning to economic actions. Companies and corporations that first and foremost see themselves as things of an economic nature – defined by the shareholders' interests as the primary motivation – therefore have a self-understanding that clearly is in conflict with the liberal, pragmatic acknowledgement of responsibility, solidarity and conscience. At the same, time it is, as mentioned, necessary to more generally, turn people's self-understanding when it comes to looking at work, value adding and meaning in life. Value pluralism can not just grow within company life, but has to be given room to grow there too.

CSR is pragmatically deemed a useful concept if it helps us challenge the fact that we all too easily reify companies and the economic conditions underlying their activities, so that we can see that they are not at all parts of a closed economic reality. Value creation is a web of different dimensions, ethical as well as economic. Corporate social responsibility has to be seen concretely as a part of the everyday, "meaning-seeking" behaviour of human beings, and not as an extraordinary phenomenon in reified organisations – in units that primarily either succeed or fail in adapting to economic laws and meeting the demands of the market. Therefore I am also sceptical to letting the debate on social responsibility circle around an extended interest model. It is difficult to imagine such interests without regarding them as something fixed and given once and for all. One should rather start with the individual as it orientates itself in life as a dynamic whole, based on its ethical sensibility and existential situation.

We definitely are facing inappropriate advertising, corrupt leadership, inexcusable working conditions and dishonest financial activities. But these are all conditions that have to be handled as part of our normal efforts to make company practices decent, regardless of which value framework these practices are based on. *Social* responsibility concerns, here and now, primarily companies and corporations as actors in a global economy with major impact when it comes to shaping our societies. Pragmatic philosophy opens our eyes to this by giving a complete perspective of economic actions as processes creating meaning that is impossible to isolate from the rest of our lives. In an approach like this, social responsibility is viewed as something more than making profit-seeking action and identity-seeking management decent. It is about the conditions of our lives – ecologically, culturally and socially.

It is my opinion that we can not welcome CSR or any other related new speech unless it affects the realities in business life understood as a part of a real democratic and liberal social life. As reinforcement of a market liberalism little open to value criticism, such new speech represents a constriction rather than an extension of our human possibilities. This can also be seen by reflecting on the basic conditions behind economic action that are woven into our near, social life. This will be further discussed, in the framework of the ethics of closeness, in the following chapter.

# Chapter 3

# Business ethics

Economic calculations in the emotional landscape of ethics

> *It could be doubted whether giving comfort to the dying is the highest util-producing activity possible in contemporary Calcutta. But, from another point of view, the dying are in an extremity that makes calculation irrelevant.*
>
> Charles Taylor

Business ethics has for a long time been encapsulated within what we can call a decision-making paradigm. The three ethical directions that characterise this area of applied ethics – modern deontological and utilitarian ethics, and also, at least to a certain degree, classical virtue ethics – have been shaped to fit the model of the determined economic actor. I will here, in the light of a fourth direction of ethics, what is in philosophy referred to as the ethic of closeness, sketch a critique that challenges the focus on ethical rules and regulations that we find in business life, and that in a deeper sense challenges all business ethics that uses stakeholder models and reciprocal thinking as a basis. Business ethics can not neglect the fact that a central part of our moral consciousness deals with a sensitivity genuinely directed towards others, a sensitivity that can not be "mastered" and surely not reframed into some form of goal directedness.

## Ethics in business

As an academic discipline – a branch of so-called applied ethics – business ethics has now found a footing within most business schools in the western world.[55] This is a process that has taken some 30-40 years and is still ongoing. And in practical life outside the academic world discussion on moral issues runs continuously, both in the media and at the levels of sectors and companies. It is often, as mentioned in Chapter I, triggered by examples of greed and definite moral violations. Seen thus, business ethics is often negatively defined – as a longing for order and decency when something has gone wrong inside a given system of action. It is far from understood as the emotional and demanding character of human interaction that exists prior to any such system. This is also mirrored in the scientific and pedagogic part of the phenomenon, since we here often circle around the so-called ethical dilemmas in business activities – situations of choices where economic and ethical demands pull in different directions. Then it is crucial to find a steady footing in order to be able to separate right from wrong action and restore order. As discussions go on, what often seems called for are definite criteria and clear regulations.

One often then resorts to one of the two main philosophical ethical directions. One either starts the search for a criterion to test the moral correctness (Kant and the categorical imperative, or Bentham/Mill and the utility principle) or one tries to anchor the respectable action in a description of the characteristics of the good human being (Aristotle and the virtues). One might even move into a direction that is both more abstract and more modern, and couple the concept of doing right with more superior reflections on justice in society (Rawls, the impartial perspective). No matter which theo-

---

[55] An overview of the history of business ethics as an academic science, both in Europe and the USA, can be found in Mahoney (1990).

retical anchoring this ethical rearmament is supposed to lead to, there will be an increased awareness of something that each and every one of us is supposed to manage. In order to be able to make good decisions everyone is supposed to manage ethical challenges almost in the same way as they are supposed to manage the work in accounting or with the multivariate methods for data analysis used in market surveys.

The idea is that one can be saved by knowledge, knowledge of general principles that can be used in any definite instance. One rarely – hardly ever – questions whether the ethical content can be handled within such a framework, within such a knowledge and resoluteness paradigm. The most basic question will always have to be if such an approach – this paradigmatic idea of the human being in business as a self-determined, well-informed acting subject – brings up what is peculiar with ethics compared to other forms of knowledge or action readiness. Therefore we need to ask: is it an ethics of resoluteness, alternatively, of calculation or principle-directed reflection, which is most in line with our most basic moral experiences and intuitions? Can an ethics of spontaneity or sensitivity describe the challenges in business life in a different and maybe richer way – and even describe entirely other moral challenges?

But most fundamentally: maybe it is time for composure when it comes to all this "talk about ethics", also in business life. Can it be there is a reason we feel the genuinely ethical can not be theorised and "talked about" in an ordinary way? According to an ethics of spontaneity and sensitivity, the ethical is directly connected to the aspect of being open to confrontation with *the unknown* and in principle un-masterable and unrestrained in close relations to other people.[56] The goal for further discussion here is to point out how such an ethic of the spontaneous and open in social meetings – at the

---

[56] A brief and very precise indication of this can be found in Thomassen (1996).

same time as it is connected to consciousness about the existential basis of the human being – challenges some of the most basic assumptions in business ethics. This concerns three mutually related conditions in particular: 1) the resource apprehension of the human being, 2) the contract apprehension of social links and 3) the regulation apprehension of moral norms and values.

## The two known routes

Let us first, before we approach the alternative in the form of an ethics of closeness, take a look at the content of the two known forms of ethics of resoluteness:

A. *The focus on right action.* In the evaluation of economically motivated choices and actions in business life the genuinely moral lies in taking a principled and neutral standing. This enables making universal judgements or being able to impartially calculate the best possible outcome. From this flows the understanding that there can be no morals without general principles, and that no action can be moral if it is not taken in the acknowledgement of the validity of such principles. Furthermore this allows for a regulation-based understanding of morals; to be moral means to uncover and follow impersonal rules. In practice we often talk about safeguarding oneself against experiencing that single actions are in conflict with established rules and approved norms of decent management. In other words: one tends to focus on whether actions and economic initiatives have a legal character.

B. *The focus on the person and personal character.* The moral evaluation of managers and employees in business life follows a picture of the good man as a whole. The role in working life has to be shaped in line with moral virtue, virtue that is given to those who wish to develop their capability and predispositions in unity with others in a community. Consideration here has to be directed towards how our economic choices fall in line with a uniform coherent picture of our identity. The goal is, fundamentally, to create a feeling of belonging to one's own life, a belonging that follows using one's wisdom and powers of judgement to balance self-interest with other forms of social and other directed action. The good is found, in other words, in serenity and inner harmony. Successfulness in terms of meeting instrumental economic demands is part of a practical reasoning where the main focus is on what possesses intrinsic value. The acknowledged meaning of a community leads to establishing an understanding of the company as a responsible moral actor, an actor with an independent and extended social responsibility – both for the employees as whole human beings and for other partners (in a wide sense) in the company's surroundings.

## Ethics of closeness as a third route[57]

In connection to this, the school of thought that is called ethics of closeness can be a stimulating and challenging "third route" in business ethics. This thinking insists that moral feelings and responsibility have their origin in everyday encounters between human beings, and that moral responsibility, therefore, will always be concretely directed towards the individual as a unique, single person. In this lies acknowledging that definite encounters are always complex, that meeting another person means standing opposite something that is a radical "otherness" – and that one consequently can not force these encounters into predefined cognitive categories without wielding

---

[57] Many will claim that the concept of ethics of closeness is deceptive, particularly when we think of the ethic presented by Løgstrup. They will, and this might be more philosophically correct, prefer the notion ontological ethics. See for instance Hansen (1996).

violence on their distinctive characteristics. Therefore the capacity for moral action presupposes a deeply emotionally based perception of the situation of The Other. "The Face" will inevitably radiate a moral appeal (Levinas)[58], a moral claim (Løgstrup).

Thus we can say what remains is the entire concept of morality understood as principle and regulation. Focus is also moved away from the resoluteness and thoughtfulness looking for a uniform coherent inner life. The focus is transferred outward. Out towards what spontaneously comes forward as morally charged, towards what is genuinely different from oneself, and what one therefore can not master but must subordinate oneself to and be challenged by. What is abandoned is more generally the idea that ethics is about what the single human being sees, recognises and wants. Human beings will always live and unfold in an existence together with others. The individual *find itself* in responsible relations from the very beginning – it forms a part of the first possible description of what it is to be a human being.

One of the most distinct analyses of this fusion of identity development and ethics in modern philosophy can be found in Zygmunt Bauman.[59] Ethics – and all emotions following moral responsibility – is not something that comes forward to us as already fully shaped persons, Bauman states. The responsibility-related emotions that come forward to and challenge *me*, are at the same time constructing the unique and complete self that this *mine-ness* refers to. Only if I let *The Other* step forward as my responsibility can I claim that I myself am an independent person. What creates the self, and what also creates the *mine-ness* of the emotions I orientate myself from, is accordingly the morally charged relationship to other people. Our idea of being human, and being one human being, rests upon this picture of

---

[58] A brief description of Levinas emphasizing of the significance of face – the definite other – to ethics, can be found in Aarnes (1997).
[59] Central in this respect is his book *Postmodern Ethics* (1996a).

taking something up, responding to something that is there already and engaging. In order to seize the reality of the definite moral ties between human beings – actually, for there to be any moral self at all coming into being – something has to *exist* as possible to confront that is not constructed by the moral self. Bauman states as follows:

> Responsibility conjures up the Face I face, but it also creates me as a moral self. Taking responsibility as if I was already responsible is an act of creation of the moral space... This responsibility which is taken "as if it was already there" is the only foundation morality can have... There is nothing necessary in being moral. Being moral is a chance which may be taken up; yet it may be also, and easily, forfeited. The point is, however, that losing the chance of morality is also losing the chance of the self.[60]

For Bauman and for Emmanuel Lévinas,[61] whom Bauman leans on, no pure individualism is able to provide a correct picture of the self and the mechanisms in the fact that the self can make emotions its own and responsibility its own. This can only be achieved through an understanding of the power in the meeting with definite others – a power that has to be considered as if it was already there. A clearer challenge to economic individualism and resoluteness as a model of responsibility can hardly be imagined.

Still, the ethical subject here is not a community member. The ethical subject is always the individual, the one to which definite claims are issued. This means that I am not my own moral master.

---

[60] Bauman (1996a, p. 75–77).
[61] Lévinas is often referred to as one of the greatest thinkers of our time, with his basic thesis of ethics as the first philosophy, where the relationship to the face is immediately ethical. For a brief introduction to his thinking, see Lévinas (1995) – a discourse on his basic claim about the relationship between human beings as ethical material. In addition the Norwegian professor of philosophy Arne Johan Vetlesen has made a good introduction to Lévinas in Vetlesen (1996a).

Ethical relations are relations that I myself do not master, but are given by something outside of me. Something that is laid down ready for me that, so to speak, gives my ethical consciousness foothold in the world. A definite and non-reducible responsibility which is directed towards me, from a definite other. Therefore, to act morally is to act one-sidedly, on behalf of The Other, without claiming retribution or reciprocity. It is in other words, phenomenologically seen, the indubitable pendant to profit-thinking and goal-oriented value creation. It concerns another concept of reality than the one that embraces the more or less balanced trades of the market.

Moreover, this moral awakening, the appeal that has its origin in The Other, is according to the ethics of closeness always radically underdefined. And this is what most clearly makes visible the difference between ethical responsibility and a contractual obligation. The content of such an obligation is provided by the contract. It is precisely agreed upon, defined through specified elements like delivery agreements and job specifications. In the role of employee or contract partner it is frighteningly easy to see oneself as completely replaceable and by that not at all unique. We can say that it is a part of the spirit of Weberian bureaucracy that it is supposed to be like this. But by that, in such a contract-based understanding of human communities, there is again created a distance, an experienced distance to other human beings, both within and outside the community. Fulfilling your function is seen as essential. This is highly antithetical to the ethics of closeness. Zygmunt Bauman states:

> ... the difference between a moral responsibility and a contractual obligation. The latter is well defined ... a contractual obligation says exactly what I am supposed to do ... I fulfil my obligations under the assumption that my counterpart fulfils his ... It is a relation of equal exchange between us ... This is all very different from the moral obligation ... Our relationship is not in any sense

symmetrical or mutual ... "Who is he and what has he done to gain the right to my services?" becomes meaningless.[62]

It is in other words not possible to justify that your moral responsibility is supposed to end where your professional function meets another's. To behave with absolute professional integrity does not at all guarantee that moral responsibility is protected. The legitimate child of the demarcation of job-functions is the experience of replaceability, and this does not harmonize very well with the concept of moral responsibility according to the ethics of closeness. The following comment by Arne Johan Vetlesen indicates this very much to the point:

> The replaceability of the individual has its standard verbal testimony in the statement: "I just did my job!" This statement is the antithesis of the ethics of closeness as it is formulated by Lévinas and Løgstrup. Instead of the person that is inalienable to The Other, who is the recipient of the appeal in the face, we find the official who has joined and disappeared into organisations ... The moral responsibility has not come along on the road.[63]

Responsibility for The Other has to be understood as something qualitatively different than a functional obligation. It is often unspoken and indeterminate. It has to be followed spontaneously, and not be calculated, determined by contract or thought. Moral responsibility is placed on me from the moment I am exposed to the appeal in the face of The Other, but what this responsibility concretely is about I have to interpret myself through empathetic insight into the situation of The Other. This is exactly what makes life as a moral

---

[62] Bauman (1996b, p. 118–119). My translation to English.
[63] Vetlesen (1996a, p. 167). My translation from Norwegian.

life-form a life in constant uncertainty, followed by a constant feeling of insufficiency. Once called to responsibility, you can never be sure if you have done right or done enough.

The ethics of closeness is first and foremost a powerful confrontation with the part of business ethics that claims a separation between personal ethics and ethics in working life. The ethics of closeness does not make any such context-limited, free positioning of will possible, nor a limitation towards a legal "Darwinistic" market ethics or a change from a sincere, personal moral alertness to act in accordance with a given rule or expectations written in contracts. Both free competition and bureaucratic impartiality are parasitic on an underlying moral consciousness. Ethics is *one*, and defined prior to social lines of demarcation and the practical organisation of society. But how can such an "economy hostile" (or in general, "discipline hostile") ethics contribute positively to clarifying the moral challenges in business life? We can start with a closer challenging of business life's engagement with rules in its moral setting.

## Immoral ethical rules

It is not seldom that morality is regarded as the same as law, and moral norms, consequently, as something that can be compared with juridical law regulations. The idea behind this must be that moral responsibility is best maintained if it is incorporated into a collective consciousness shaped by rules that in the clearest possible way delineate between right and wrong, between what is imperative, allowed and forbidden. Rules are prepared in order to create a common understanding of situations and by that make clear responsibility – its content and scope. One can of course say that one can not blame actors in business life for seeking operational solutions when it also comes to "the work with ethics". The good thing about explicit rules of conduct is of course that they are visible and put problematic moral affairs on the business agenda. They can be directly perceived as working conditions that one must act in accordance with. And by way of these rules one can possibly bring ethics into focus in every day work as well, and not only at conferences and in speeches and annual reports. Attempting to integrate the rules into everyday practice, one may claim, is always better than trying to raise praxis up towards brilliant goals and unlimited visions.

But, and here we have quite a considerable "but": if we are to take the ethics of closeness seriously, ethical rules are not suited to capturing any real moral value – the true moral responsibility. Rules create security and convenience – they are replacements for the spontaneous, unrestrained and demanding in the complexity of the manifestation of life that characterises meetings between human beings. Rules are meant to create agreeability with common, spoken and reasonable claims, with general norms that are to be followed for their own sake, or in order to preserve the general social order, not because one sincerely wants to serve The Other. That moral claims are in this way *formulated* can therefore be said to be a sign, a sign that something has already reached a crisis. Ethical rules can therefore, just as much as positive moral alertness, be seen as an expression of a collective conscience determined for crisis. In other words, what has already reached crisis has to be the individual sensitivity, the moral perception.

A re-establishing of this sensitivity, this openness to The Other and the unmanageable, can not happen as a collective movement. It is not at all about establishing good laws and rules for the common good – it is about not obscuring the appeal of The Other as it emerges for the individual. We can put it as follows: to be *together with* others can very well be regulated by rules; to be there *for* The Other can not at all. This is the true core of the ethics of closeness. It should therefore be an awakening for an at least apparently ethically oriented business life that ethical rules can be considered morally suspect. In fact, action solely based on rules can be said to be morally blameworthy. Løgstrup states quite explicitly that to argue for an action only from a general moral rule is unethical:

> But is that kind of arguing ethical? Is it not in fact actually unethical? I would claim that it is. In the general argumentation, moralizing happens for its own sake, in other words becomes moralism, which is how morality becomes immoral.[64]

Here we see a clear parallel to Max Weber's, and later Jurgen Habermas', considerations of how instrumental rationality colonises increasingly more of our social life world. One of the expressions of this rational thinking Weber worried about was exactly the strictly rule-based action we find with bureaucrats, where formalisation and standardisation of decisions leads to systematic deprivation of responsibility for the overall results. In other words, a way of action where considerations of efficiency are blinding, where rules are followed simply for the sake of following rules. To follow duties, rules or expressed norms is, in Løgstrup's understanding of ethics, an example of something "morally introverted".

## The moral foundation of rationality

We can approach these basic points by also looking at the action fixation that characterises the view of rationality in economics. A focus on unconditional external action is obviously a misdirection in the light of the ethics of closeness, with its focus on self-defining moments, expressions of life and the supporting elements of our social life that are made visible in face-to-face meetings. At the same time there is no doubt that we, in business life, have to act within functionally restricted areas – functions that are supposed to pro-

---

[64] Løgstrup (1972, p. 36). My translation from Danish.

mote action rationality. It is therefore difficult to acknowledge how The Other rightfully can claim anything from me, if it is not reasoned exactly in such an exercise of function. Consequently claims detached from convention and contractual rights and rules of the game, easily acquire an irrational, that is to say, unreasoned, touch. So what one does is create a belief that "one takes ethics seriously" by producing guidelines on how to best possibly nurture relations to different stakeholders, on how they deserve to be treated, given their relative contributions to the company's value creation.

Business ethics is, with that, deeply anchored in an idea of reciprocity, in the idea of rationality of action that operates from so-called contribution and reward balances. But the aforementioned irrational touch only belongs to an economic reality. According to the ethics of closeness we are not first and foremost independent, desirous and acting individuals, equipped with a set of interests or demands others can meet or fail to meet, and thereafter moral actors. We first of all belong to a moral reality – ethical responsibility is integral to the acting and knowing subject. Ethics, the responsibility, is *the first*. This is pointed out by Lévinas when he says that ethics is first philosophy. The fact that one can be the recipient of an ethical claim is, as we have seen, included in the earliest possible definition of oneself as a human being – it is the defining element in human ontology. Precisely this aspect must be said to be a very strange element related to the dominant business ethical thinking of today, where it seems to be taken for granted that subjectivity and subjective interests come first and define the economic sphere of social interaction.

And this *first* can of course be neither rational nor irrational; it simply *is*. Morality is in other words incalculable and arational. The meeting with The Other can not be rationalised, neither the one (through rules) nor the other way (through economic calculation). The manifestations of life that appear in the meetings between human beings are spontaneous and sovereign. That the manifestations of life are spontaneous means exactly that they are made and lived up to without calculation, without ulterior motive, and also without reference to more basic moral duties. And according to the Danish philosopher and theologian Knud E. Løgstrup, it is precisely the spontaneity characterizing these manifestations of life that represents ethics at its best. That ethics is sovereign, points to the fact that it always comes before choices of action – it is an expression of the social life that, in the Løgstrup's words, "is already there".

Expressions or manifestations of life are therefore at the same time offering life a direction and a strong demand of moral character. The intuitive feeling that comes in advance of rationality, calculation and one's own action, is therefore at the same time a feeling of the irreplaceable life conditions and the moral obligations we encounter in our social reality. It follows from what has been said so far, that a definite relationship exists between the ethical basic phenomena, the moral appeal and the spontaneous expressions of life on the one side, and the calculations often done in advance of economic choices on the other side. The claim and the ethical basic phenomena manifest themselves ahead of, and independent of, the calculation and constitution of will in one's calculation of the best possible outcome from an economic perspective.

Or to put it more succinctly: business relations are maintained by award balances. Ethics – the basic ethical phenomena – is part of keeping alive the world where business relations are at all *possible*. Ethics is a part of existing, of how the world reveals itself to us – it is not a (contractual) construction we have chosen to maintain for reasons of utility within the world. Trust, for instance, is not first of all favourable, but inevitable. Ethics comes *before* any consideration of favourability. Being sensitive to moral intuitions and following ethical obligations comes before any realization of economic rationality. This is exemplarily presented in a central statement made by Løgstrup:

What can not be rationalised are our manifestations of life, trust, openness, indignation, compassion, hope ... They create the constants in our life ... They are not irrational; they are of an origin that comes before the difference between rationality and irrationality.[65]

Since the moral claim is something that comes from the outside, has its roots in The Other and not oneself, and therefore can not be governed by one's own practical sense, it can not be calculated either. It can not be placed in one's own structure and description of the alternatives of action. Morality is given ahead of calculation. Calculation can therefore only to *some extent* address the content of the moral claim. Or, mildly interpreted, we can say that this shows the difference between economic calculation on the one hand, and ethical calculation on the other, where ethical calculation is characterised by the fact that a goal can set limits to which means that can be chosen to realize it. In Kantian terms, one would say that duty comes ahead of one's own evaluation and reasoning. Or rather, again lending an ear to Zygmunt Bauman:

> ... morality is endemically and irredeemably *non-rational* – in the sense of not being calculable, hence not being presentable as following impersonal rules ... I am moral *before* I think.[66]

Ethics presents a counter light that both challenges and makes possible action in a reality that will always be a moral reality. It challenges by continuously asking questions about our ability to define ourselves from within, by setting the limits of what we can master. It *makes possible* by representing the fundamental, and at the same time

---

[65] Løgstrup (1983, p. 119). My translation from Danish.
[66] Bauman (1996a, p. 61).

delicate, basis that all social life is founded upon. Behind such an understanding of our values lies of course a basic scepticism to any concept of radical free choices – the more existentialist idea that we ourselves create our values through the choices we make. Seen in this way, the ethics of closeness presented by Løgstrup is a "reverse" position, as argued by Hansen: "The basis of values is not created through the choices people make, but is a condition for our choices."[67] The reciprocity that counts as a norm in economic reality is therefore a special and superficial form of the *interdependence* – the deep, reciprocal human dependence – that characterises the relationship between human beings in general. As Løgstrup says:

> What is characteristic of human existence is that we are mutually dependant upon each other, and the dependence goes so deep, that without it our existence would not at all be human.[68]

## From the small to the large – the inevitability of system criticism

That we are supposed to be touched by the "small" meetings and close relationships with other human beings (a part of being conscious to basic conditions under which we live), implies that we also need to discuss the characteristics of the large structures within which we act. The ethics of closeness, in others words, begins in the social micro cosmos, and then moves over to the macro problems: what about the system? What kind of attitudes and actions does it stimulate? Does it accomodate or shut out the appeal of The Other, does it thereby protect and enhance rather than diminish individual

---

[67] Hansen (1996, p. 155). My translation from Norwegian.
[68] Løgstrup (1961, p. 137), cited and commented on by Hansen (1996, p. 105). My translation from Danish.

sensitivity? Does it make me fit to actually see and be there *for* The Other, or does it hamper The Other's appearance?

We therefore need to constantly keep watch that The Other does not vanish, not only behind the self-interest-based pursuit of revival in the market world of competition, but also behind the objectification that follows from administration and planning needs. Objectification, that is, in the shape of both the inevitable expert-based division of labour and the reification of the tools and categorisations of analytical strategy work. It is not only egoism and greed that are the enemies of the moral impulse. Just as frightening are the responsibility reducing effects of the by-products of instrumental reason that categorize and rank people based on their expediency or their potential for profit. Vetlesen states:

> Finally, we need to be careful in how we use our language in describing other people. Letting persons be anonymous representatives of categories or collectives can be a dangerous step in the direction of regarding the persons as replaceable and without value. [69]

In other words, obscuring the unique and challenging of the individual can be done just as easily by linguistic and thought-based barriers as by physical lines of demarcation. In this way our use of economic and management language can alienate us by construing as strange The Other as a source of unconditioned responsibility. Economic language can easily lay a mist of tastefulness and utility over humans as fellow-beings. But at the same time, in direct line with the concrete nature of this ethics, it is also disturbing that, in the name of efficiency, the faces also vanish in the physical sense – post offices are shut down, shops flock to the Internet, the physical locations of banks are close to redundant. It is the *human presence* that

---

[69] Vetlesen (1996a, p. 172). My translation from Norwegian

is about to be wiped out when the face systematically is wiped out. What consequently is de-emphasised is the inevitable complexity in concrete meetings with others, the irresistible and challenging in these meetings. And it is the useful information, the idea of economic mutuality and the "what's in it for me?"-attitude that easily comes as a replacement. Rational and efficiency definitely improve – but in a very narrow sense.

So here we definitely find a track of an underlying critical attitude to the growth and innovation condensed market society. How do we behave towards the world around us – which fundamental attitude is dominant? Will the technology-driven development in the e-society make our treatment of the world calculating, instrumental, technical and categorising? Will the commandment "learn to filter the relevant information" make us shut ourselves into our progressive self-interest? Is the social world something we need to master, and not something that we feel ourselves exposed to? Do we feel hit by the now fairly well-known graffiti: "Technology is the answer. What is the question?" We may therefore ask:

> But where will such digital innovation end? A change where flexibility replaces identity. Where news replace closeness. Where *what* and *how* in the flood of information replaces *why*.[70]

The ideal-typical calculation of profit that we find in business life shows us par excellence the individual as it takes possession of the world. The other way around, says Levinas, is ethics. Ethics is characterised by a "reverse intentionality". I am called to responsibility – before choices, before thinking. The "I" is no longer the first person. Ethics – expressed by The Other – is inevitably a disturbance, a tur-

---

[70] Truls Lie, editorial in the Norwegian newspaper *Morgenbladet*, 15th May 2001. My translation from Norwegian.

bulence in the flow of the life of the individual, something that does not quite fit. And we may add: perhaps particularly not in the world as it is revealed as an economic reality. It is not as a resource that The Other appears as a moral figure, but quite simply as a fellow human being. In the ethics of closeness the way to reflect on this "why", indicated in the quotation above, will always and inevitably be via the concrete, tangible and perceptible Meeting. If the Meeting is something very infrequent, remote, then so is reflection.

The comprehension of the human being as a resource belongs to an ethics of action and resoluteness, an ethics that easily can be regarded as at the basis of economic reality and the contractual understanding of human relations that comes with it, and that, therefore, is far from the ethics of sensitivity and closeness. Thus it is not difficult to understand that the ethics of closeness has found its application first in the ethical dimension of health and medical care. The core of the ethics of closeness appears as most relevant and appropriate when people meet face to face, and in particular when one party is physically, and often also psychically vulnerable. This is nevertheless no valid argument for limiting this kind of ethical reflection to one form of applied ethics. The ethic of closeness forms a part of basic ethics and has consequently a potential to contribute to the shaping of any area-specific ethics.

## Conclusion – ethics before business

Will this necessarily end up in a rather classical situation where ethics and business are opposite poles – in a conflict of a logical and insoluble character? Can business never be ethical? Will a profit-oriented attitude forever be a parasite on the ethical foundation of our social existence? In other words, is the concept of "business ethics" itself, as Peter F. Drucker so forcefully expressed already more than twenty years ago: "the most improper"?

We can at least say this: the ethical reflection that follows from this "third line of thought" reminds us of limits. It reminds us about the absolute character of our moral responsibility, and not least about the reality of moral claims – that ethics is included in what is real for us as complete human beings.[71] This understanding of ethics will remind us that there exists a *before*; the rich, complex and demanding something that manifests itself before the choice, before the calculation, before analysis and before our planning. In no other ethical understanding can we find such a strong and sincere denial of the economic reality as the "real reality". Even though it is of course not meant to cover the complete spectrum of our ethical problems, this line of thought can be a rich corrective to the knowledge and mastering attitude that to a great extent characterises the ethics of business today.[72]

Where we see this most clearly and with most relevance to business practice, is in relation to the phenomenon of trust. Trust as a phenomenon does not exist related, in a conditioned form, to a given, internal goal in praxis. When it comes to claims like trust, business life in praxis must be considered at the same level as any other human activity. It presupposes them, with no clear purpose. Even the action of defining – and not to mention agreeing upon – a goal and a plan, presumes that such can be done based on a foundation of manifestations of life with inherent moral qualities. Thus trust does not only constitute an advantageous feature in society and in the building of relations, it

---

[71] Our humanity and identity are closely and insolubly attached to what Taylor (1985a and 1985b) calls strong evaluations. The relationship between Taylor's communitarian ethics and the ethics of closeness can, in very simplified terms, be presented as follows: The manifestations of life and the moral claims described in the ethics of closeness are part of the ethical basis that shows us where – in which situations – strong evaluations are imperative and give meaning and direction to our action.

[72] The perhaps most obvious blind spot in the ethics of closeness is the moral challenge attached to the management of nature. The ethics of closeness is basically concerned with the relationship between human beings. Animals, plants and natural resources have no direct position in this picture.

... is a basic feature of linguistic communication itself. One does not need to be trustful to expose oneself to another, one only need approach another human being.[73]

To sum up, we can say that there are two main elements in the understanding of the ethics that dominates business that stand in sharp contrast to the ethics of closeness. Insistence on establishing The Other, the concrete demand, as a moral measure, is incompatible with the following two conditions:

1. To understand ethical and social responsibility completely based on a model of stakeholders' interest (what we above have noted as the thought of contractual relationships and mutuality)
2. To believe that this responsibility can be attended to by developing and living up to ethical rules (what we have presented as the typical attempt to clarify responsibility, the juridification and the idea of convenience).

The ethics of closeness points out a completely different direction. Business ethics can not correctly be described as ethics for business. It is ethics *before* business – an ethics on this side of economic calculation and the bureaucratic division of work. It reminds us that concepts like resources, efficiency, rational choice, management and managing are concepts that belong to a form of life that unfolds within the framework of a series of basic conditions for human life. It reminds us that no moral understanding can find footing within a subject that pursues an epistemological or economic distance to the world and its human inhabitants.

---

[73] Andersen (1996, p. 61). My translation from Norwegian. For a thorough indication of the role of trust as a spontaneous expression of life with a fundamental significance for economic activity, in particular in a Keynesian perspective, see Aasland (1999).

## Chapter 4

# What is a company?
## About value communities and value pluralism

> *Economists and economic theorists naturally tend to look at systems and theories of systems, while ethicists tend to look at individual behaviour, its motives and consequences. Neither of these approaches is suitable for business ethics.*
>
> Robert C. Solomon

## The company as a social construction

The question of what a company is can not be understood purely theoretically, beyond any historical and cultural context. Like any other element of social reality, companies are socially constructed. This means that companies, and their goals, are subject to genuine change because of the changing (collective) self-understanding of human beings. Companies are what they are based on our socially anchored search for meaning and culturally based understanding of our own economic life. We can not clarify what a company is without clarifying what it means to be a social human being. This also means that a company is primarily an element of a "pure" business economical reality so as long as it is understood as such. In this chapter I will challenge the economic-theoretical view of the company along lines drawn up by, among others, the American philosopher Robert C. Solomon. A central theme here is a presentation of – including an indication of the limits of – a community oriented understanding of the company.

A company can of course be identified and described as something actual, something that implies that we, in our understanding, freeze – or objectify and even reify – the structures, rules and dominant ways of thinking that are manifested in the company at a given moment of time. A company can also be described dynamically as a development in such institutionalized structures. But as an arena for human action – a complex set of practices forming self-understanding and self-defining subjects – it can not primarily be understood as such, in a purely theoretical way. From a perspective of action the important point is to be reminded that companies are social constructions, and that companies therefore – like any other institution – are intersubjective praxis areas that are continuously reconstructed by self-interpreting subjects both inside and outside their borders. As Thor Øyvind Jensen states:

> Organisations are, in their inner core, social constructions that are carried by the unity, enthusiasm and interests of human beings. The buildings, the products and the cash flows are only indications that they exist ... It is the workers, the managers, the customers and the owners that through trust, enthusiasm and different feelings of commitment choose the activities that are coordinated to what is sensed, seen and described as "the organisation". [74]

In this we see a rather uncontroversial social constructivism. According to this way of thinking, organising and company life are most deeply regarded as process-oriented "sense-making", not efficient adjustment to given goals. This is in line with the pragmatic thinking in Chapter 2: human beings are never confronted with objective economic facts (profit goals) and market laws (competition) to which they just have to adjust and adapt. The human being is free,

---

[74] Jensen (2005, p. 225). My translation from Norwegian.

not only on the surface through its concrete possibilities to choose among several available products, investments and jobs, but by being able to interpret and relate to its possibilities – and by that, to challenge and go beyond them.

The economic concept of rationality – that is not derived from the different meaning-constituting norms and values that shape different social arenas (for example, the family, friendships, the market, politics, science, the arts), but is ascribed to the individual in advance of its participation in these arenas – is consequently strange to this basic statement.[75] The context-free and institution-independent rationality – the "super-rationality" that only refers to the so called subjective preferences of the individual, its information on alternatives and ability to calculate – break with the perspectives in the constructivist tradition that aim at sensitivity to the concrete and practice-related.

The purpose here, based on such a consciousness of perspective, is to sketch a challenge to what I call the economic view of the company – a basic interpretation in the business economical sciences that in particular manifests itself in so-called economic organisational theory. Rather simplified, this view says that a company is *actually* or *truly* a contract-based collection of self-interests in the service of profit. The view of the human being that dominates the theory is materialistic, since the human being here is an "actor" with "stable and transitive preferences" who "chooses freely" among existing combinations of goods – the question whether these choices and preferences actually are the individual's own, based on its own comprehension and by that an expression of true individuality, is not touched on in this theory. The conceptualisation and lacking depth in the understanding of the situation is not discussed. And consequently the rationality is a pure, instrumental rationality.

---

[75] In the deepest sense, this means that (economic) rationality can be said to consist of some advance criteria, and not attached to a wider and more open concept of reasonable action.

Another way to put this is to say that the goal or motive is either objectively given in and by the system or purely subjectively given by the (non-rational) emotions, that is, in any case beyond the domain of reason, discourse and cooperation. Economic theorists that claim that the company "in reality" – or "actually" or "basically" – is determined by contractual relations, in other words, because of their materialistic human ontology, have a well-developed blindness to other, possibly rich, perspectives, perspectives prone to recognize economic power and to uncover narrow conceptions of value creation.

First of all, what we are discussing here includes a basic and formal philosophical point: a rejection of the belief that it is possible to identify something as an "absolutely real" human world, in the sense of an inherent reality following laws of development. If the human world of action and meaning is socially constructed, there is no objective reality behind the processes where this world unfolds. Secondly, I will sketch an alternative perspective of the company as a collective and social unity, where the division between economic and non-economic (virtue) elements is central, and where the starting point is the comprehensive view of the human being as primarily an acting, emotive being. In all this the company is seen as a social value community indicating value pluralism. And seen in this way, paid work is not primarily structured around egocentric utility actions, but rather utility actions can be seen as one type of meaning creation that originates in the human ability to act expressively and morally responsibly in business life.

In short, rationality of action is not attached to how well we maximise our given self-interest, but how well we have developed the understanding of what an adequate attitude to different goods will be. Such an extensive and diverse concept of rationality therefore allows for several different sub-categories, not all of which share the assumption of action based on fixed preferences, and that generally share neither the result orientation nor the maximising assumptions in economic theory. The obvious and deep contrast between economic rationality and an apprehension that has its basis in pluralistic value theory can be clearly seen in the following citation of the American philosopher Elisabeth Anderson:

> An expressive theory defines rational action as action that adequately expresses our rational attitudes toward people and other intrinsically valuable things ... the expressive theory opens up an alternative basis for ranking actions besides the value of their consequences. Actions are ranked according to how well they express our rational evaluations.[76]

The main difference lies in the fact that rationality is attached to attitudes and value evaluations — what is reasonable or fair in different contexts — rather than to actions satisfying a certain formula. Such an interpretation of rationality can, as mentioned, be easily attached to a pragmatic, non-dualistic theory of social construction of meaning. On such a basis an extended value consciousness in the area of business ethics can also grow, a consciousness that is embraced by concepts like corporate social responsibility and corporate citizenship. This concept of corporate citizenship embraces two mutually clarifying conditions: 1) the company as a responsible unit in society, and 2) the company as a community of and for subjects in their quest for meaning. It is this concept of the *human being in the company* that I will try in the following section to circle around and describe, and claim is conclusive for an understanding of the company as a (part of a) changeable social reality.

---

[76] Anderson (1993, p. 17–22).

## Community and critical individualism

To regard company life as an expression of real value community will of course break with the aforementioned view of the company that we especially find in modern agent-principal theory and transaction cost economics, where the company is only an abstract concept referring to the group of contractual relations that comprise the human basis of profit. The company is a kind of internal, modified market where authority has partly replaced the "natural" price-mechanism as a mode of coordination. The company is a modified result of the fact that one sees pure market relations between individual actors as too costly. Therefore a company in this view is just a technical solution to a coordination problem, where what is to be coordinated are given self-interests. We can say that this represents a form of scientific nominalism, where only the single self-interests are seen as real and the company is only seen as an abstraction, a purely theoretical concept that does not capture something of collective nature with interest-forming power.

To see a real value community consequently implies that we relate to the company as something *qualitatively different* from what it is according to such an economic approach. Communities appear only when we shift from seeing contracts and mutual terms of trade, to seeing whole human beings that seek belonging and meaningful expression of their ideals of the good life. In other words, when we see human beings that experience the possibility to integrate their efforts in working life into the overall picture of themselves, without too high a degree of internal conflict, an institution where a wide range of values are explicitly made real both in words and through action. The idea of value communities therefore does not build on an anti- or non-individualism, but on an individualism that is unfastened from the instrumental rational paradigm, and instead is seen as part of a non-materialistic view of the human. This we can call a critical individualism that systematically questions how the individual develops its self-interest in different manners through relating, linguistically and bodily, in social situations charged with meaning.

In such a perspective it is of course too narrow to see the company only as profit-making machinery that in its pursuit of profit– practically as an additional benefit – should also acknowledge certain ethical "limitations". Ethics "lies in" the organisations from the very beginning, not as limitations, but as integrated goals and ideals for the communal tasks the human being takes part in. It also involves a challenge to the fact that competition is supposed to be the basic principle of business life, since cooperation is introduced as just an important and substantial aspect. This also has evident consequences when it comes to which concrete ethical obligations the different parties of business life can be said to hold, something Lucas points out thus:

> Contrary to present perceptions, business is fundamentally a cooperative activity … In negotiating wages the employer's and employee's interests are opposed; but the immediate opposition is largely subsumed under a long-term profitable partnership… and the market rate can be unfair; we can justly criticize the employer who pays starvations wages, even though he can find desperate workers ready to work for a pittance, and trade unions which drive industries into bankruptcy through their exorbitant wage demands."[77]

In such a view the company is an organic whole where people are shaped and shape each other through common efforts and intersubjective reality interpretation in a large range of areas. To understand communities is therefore first and foremost to understand social

---

[77] Lucas (2003, p. 18 and 24).

acting, intersubjectivity and moral virtues, before one sees individual smartness, subjective preferences, conflicts and limiting duties. Arne Johan Vetlesen points out how ending a membership in a working community often turns out:

> People who loose their jobs often miss, not the work itself, but the colleagues. They also miss the experience of being part of a community — and for better or worse — being seen by other human beings. To fall outside working life can turn out to be like falling into invisibility ...[78]

What might therefore be the most important part of any project aimed at seeing the company as a real community is that such a perspective might point at the fact that life is to be lived as a whole, and not an assemblage of independent components in the shape of different roles. For it is unquestionably so, as stated by Robert C. Solomon, that:

> ... one of the problems of traditional business thinking is our tendency to isolate our business or professional roles from the rest of our lives.[79]

To see the individual's connection to the company as a contractual relationship undoubtedly isolates its real self from its contribution to economic value creation. To move our eyes from profitable contracts entered between independent parties towards real value communities demands a direct confrontation with economic individualism (here emphasising *economic* and not individualism) — the focus on the individual that places the single individual as a carrier of the

---
[78] Henriksen/Vetlesen (2000, p. 115).
[79] Solomon (1997, p. 216).

social world by virtue of her instrumental rationality. A business ethics focusing on the human-being-in-the-company must have its origin in other premises than those which provide the foundation for an exchange perspective on the market, actually on the whole society, and by that provide the basis for an external view of the relationship between the individual and social life.[80]

Ethical theories that grow from the idea of historical traditions and community we often call communitarian. Being communitarian means perceiving ethical values as essentially attached to the existence of concrete cultural communities of which individuals inevitably are a part.[81] Ethical values are not given and universal, something that without friction – that is, interpretation – can be transferred from culture to culture or from one historical era to another. Ethical values have to do with how the individuals see, interpret and value the world in concrete social contexts. The majority of different forms of virtue ethics are, in this respect, communitarian, by emphasising the virtues at the same time as they focus on functioning well within the historically given practices in which the individual acts.[82]

The confrontation with economic individualism is therefore in many ways visible in virtue ethical business ethics. One here tries to establish a view of business based on a concept of virtue and the good life, and not efficiency considerations based on separate means and goals. One of the leading virtue ethicists in business ethics, the American Robert C. Solomon, undoubtedly wants to make an issue

---

[80] For a thorough introduction to the relation between individuality and sociality, through a concept of rationality (and freedom), see Hegge (2003).
[81] For a brief and simple introduction to the concept of communitarianism, see Vetlesen (1996b). For a wider philosophical discussion of communitarian versus universal ethics, see Rasmussen (1990).
[82] However, all virtue ethics are not completely attached to a historical and cultural framework in this way. Aristotle's ethics is one example of an ethics focusing on virtue that at the same time means to say something objective – that is, general and universal – about the goodness and happiness of the human being.

out of the narrow understanding of the individual manifest in economic thinking and business, and by that the modern philosophical subjectivism upon which it is based. He wants to exchange our concept of the individual and individuality with an Aristotelian concept of the practically engaged and socially anchored human being, something that obviously will have a large impact on the view of the company as a social unit.

The modern Judaeo-Christian and duty and consequentiality ethics have divided the individual from the community, and in addition established an understanding of morality as something in chronic contrast to positive meaning-seeking and joyful expressions of life. In relation to this, Solomon points out, we need to stimulate ethical thinking that is about the practical life as a whole, and that examines our expressive, meaningful action in different communities. Both moral and non-moral considerations and characteristics merge in the concept of human virtues, he claims. In business life it is for example just as important to have non-moral virtues, such as a sense of humour and charm, as the typically moral virtues like honesty and moderation. And it is from the virtues we have to evaluate the normative status of business life in society, since it is by them we function well as whole social beings. Business life is that which contributes to the good by giving human beings a positive value foundation, a sense of entirety and possibilities for socially responsible self-realisation through virtuous emotion and action.

Business ethics must take this seriously by acknowledging it as the basis of the discipline and not be entrenched in a negative understanding of ethics as limitations to a "more free" profit-seeking action:

> Business ethics is too often conceived as a set of impositions and constraints, obstacles to business behaviour rather than the motivating force of that behaviour ... the Aristotelian framework tells us that it is cooperation and not an isolated individual sense of

self-worth that defines the most important virtues... Business is, above all, a social activity ... The bottom line of the Aristotelian approach to business ethics is that we have to get away from both the traditional individualistic ethics and "bottom line" thinking.[83]

The human being does not define itself via itself alone, but via its social participation and belonging to different communities. Here the framework of economic individualism is broken apart, both by focusing on collective action and also by pointing out that individual, "personal" action happens within the framework of a community, within, broadly speaking, an institutionalized and socially constructed reality. A virtue ethical confrontation with the individualistic economic paradigm is therefore also a confrontation with what we can call the bottom-line-tyranny in business ethics, that one focuses solely on how different processes and initiatives affect economic profit, where the bottom line is an independent goal and not internally connected to the activities and actions that create the goal's value

## The company as praxis

The core of this community perspective is therefore the acknowledgement that business, above all, is a social activity construing our sense of meaning and reality. The relation between company and individual is not seen here as a question of mutual profit (the balance of contribution and reward) in a market world that follows its own laws, but business life is seen as a self-justifying praxis where the profit motive is subordinate to – has to be understood from the perspective of – the human quest for meaning.

The human being as a unique, independent individual with *its own* goals for self-realisation, is however a modern idea that we can not

---

[83] Solomon (1997, p. 217–224).

escape. The relevant question is not *if* the human being is, or should be, engaged in self-realisation – that is, its own individuality – but how and on what basis this happens and can best be understood. A basic virtue ethical insight is that the self-realising individual stands in a strong and necessary relation to social and moral communities. Culture and sociality do not represent the individual's surroundings, factors that may hamper action – they are the individual's inescapable foundation and value horizon. That the company can be part of this, as a community, a normative anchoring of the self-realisation of the individual and not just a "place" for display of economic forces, is not an impossible idea.

In modern society one can indeed claim that work, above all, is the arena of self-realisation. This is where the individual is supposed to display its capabilites as an individual, with the necessary distance from the family and the private sphere. The self-realisation happens in rooms where the knowledge and the abilities of the individual are put on trial, and where the individual can experience that it really is a responsible *self* towards which all demands, challenges, mastering and profit norms are directed. Though we must not be misled into believing that the individual can not realise itself until the close and committing social ties are abolished, or parenthetically, a "real" optional attachment to social life takes its place. The most clarifying interpretation of self-realisation in working life prevails if we regard the company as consisting of a different form of self-justifying praxis, and not as a value neutral place defined and thriving through external relations.

In order for us to see the company as praxis in Aristotelian terms, we need to tone down the perspective that describes the company primarily as a manufacturing unit – a more or less accidental economic construction for production. We need to focus on the elements – the relations, processes and activities – in business life that can constitute something independently valuable, something self-justifying, in the lives and actions of the people constructing it. We need, in other words, to focus just as much on the *internal goods* of business life as on the more primitive external goods that economic theory systematically emphasises:

> Loyalty, honesty and integrity might not be necessary for the achievement of the external goods of a corporation, namely more money, but they are essential to achieving and enjoying the internal goods of such activities, goods such as friendship, a sense of belonging, and self-realisation.[84]

These virtues of loyalty, honesty and integrity are in other words not definable relative to something external, to a virtue and action independent picture of company success. They are themselves constituent parts of success, the good life, simply fostering the good qualities of the human being as a part of, and not simply means to, functioning well, also in business life. The company can be experienced as praxis if there in company life can be found zones for expressing qualitatively different rational attitudes to things and people with independent value. In other words, if company life promotes our pluralistic freedom through giving access to a wide spectrum of social spheres, a wide spectrum of contexts where we can adequately express our genuinely different attitudes. Here we can lean on a basic Aristotelian idea: harmony and happiness is internally connected to functioning well as a human being and is not an external, generic goal at which we can consciously aim. Happiness is nothing in itself, but, for example, a personal experience of ecstatic joy disconnected from its source. It can only be understood in the light of our efforts when we as acting subjects try to contribute to social activities with intrinsic value. Besides, happiness includes feeling whole, including as a

---

[84] Statman (1997, p. 25).

part of the productive life in a company, in the interchange among different fields of praxis:

> What is important is rather the place of a virtue (along with other virtues) in the living of a meaningful, fulfilling life, and what is important for a business virtue is its place in a productive, meaningful life in business. And this does not simply mean, "how does it contribute to the bottom line" but rather, does it contribute to the social harmony of the organisation? Does it manifest the best ideals of the organisation? Does it render an employee or manager "whole" or does it tear a person to pieces ...?[85]

We here touch the idea that there should be limits to our direct target focus if we wish to find deep joy in life and keep our personalities intact. It is here virtue ethical thinking most clearly diverges from an explicitly calculating and outcome-directed thinking such as we find in utilitarianism. We have seen that Solomon pointed out that friendship is one of the internal goods associated with business life. To act friendly, however, can be understood in two rather different ways: either acting with a target of creating or keeping a friendship, or acting in a friendly spirit. The latter is what is most compatible with virtue ethics, while the former belongs to utilitarian thinking. Within a virtue ethical understanding such things as friendship are not things that are to be accomplished or achieved. It is not a part of a logic of performing, of acting clever. Friendship should exist in a relation qualified by certain emotional and moral qualities, which of course will in turn qualify an organisation where such behavior is possible and appreciated.

To act thoughtfully, honestly and in a friendly spirit does in other

---

[85] Solomon (1997, p. 219). The concept-duality internal and external goods originate from the moral philosopher Alasdair MacIntyre and his communitarian ethics (1985).

words connect actions directly to one's character, and it is this understanding of action that is included as an ideal in the business ethics Solomon puts forward. The company should therefore be seen as an institution where people are allowed to act in line with their personal character and judgement and are not treated as pieces of an administrative embodiment of a given decision model, where action is always justified in the end as part of a profit-seeking strategy. Or to put it another way: a company is also a social space where rational actions have to have their origin in a deeper expressive rationality, one that expresses what one is committed to as a whole person.

The moment we move our eyes in the direction of seeing profit as "at least the most basic demand", the concept of the human being as the "company's main resource" or "human capital" becomes clearer, and at the same time the picture of the human being, both as a corporate citizen and as ethically responsible, becomes more blurred. And the division between these theoretical perspectives obviously has practical consequences, for example when it comes to how we view and handle evasion and lack of work motivation among employees. In mainstream (so-called neo-classical) economic theory, two types of parameters will be seen as relevant: monitoring, close follow-up and control, and economic incentives. But this will be a move in the wrong direction if we look at the problem from a community perspective. Here, such instruments can easily aggravate the problem by creating additional alienation in the working environment.

The point in relation to responsible action can not be to support the understanding of the individual and the company as locked in a basic conflict of interests, but has to be to build a bridge over the wedge that might have grown through a more thorough *socialisation* in the company. Tight supervision and efficient incentives on the one hand, and socialisation on the other, therefore belong to two different worlds of human resource management. In one world the human beings are isolated individuals that act on their own, from a self-defined self-interest. In the other human beings are first and foremost members of groups and cultures where actions in the deepest sense are shaped at the collective level.

## The struggle for market power – and the power of defining concepts

An important part of any attempt to change perspective is to take a close look at language and the reality-creating power of language. The basic point is that language is not just a communication device, but that it, as Ferraro, Pfeffer and Sutton remark: "shapes what people notice and ignore, and what they believe is and is not important."[86] How we describe reality affects how we act in it. We will take a more general look into the power of economic language in Chapter 5 – here we discuss business language in organizational practice. And Solomon's attempt to understand business in virtue ethical terms is basically an attempt to create, or at least aspire to, a new and different business language:

> Solomon has made an interesting attempt in preparing business ethics as virtue ethics, underlining the community idea. The attempt develops as a sharp confrontation with the language used in business, that he means is run by subversive "macho myths and metaphors"... Solomon claims that many of the problems in the business world can be attributed to this ingrained, but deeply misleading use of language that presents business in a bad light and creates unfortunate pressure that actually promotes "hostile, uncaring and ultimately destructive behaviour".[87]

---

[86] Ferraro/Pfeffer/Sutton (2005, p. 9).
[87] Asheim (1997, p. 55). My translation from Norwegian. The direct reference to Solomon is found in Solomon (1993, p. 22).

The unfortunate language is therefore a language that presents and stimulates us to act in a jungle where the "laws of the jungle" are applied, a "war" where what is important is fighting to win (the favour of the investors or the customers), a "game" where victory is all that matters – where one either "kills or is killed". Furthermore, we are speaking here of a language that is pervaded by metaphors that also create a picture of the market as a machine or a mechanism that works according to inevitable laws. This macho language with its war and win-or-clear-off metaphors, Salomon states, is a way of interpreting and creating reality that might just as much distort and efface as it might describe and clarify humans as responsible beings. A company's inner life can, as we have seen, be put into completely other and far less hostile and alienating frameworks. The downside of the rough competition metaphor is that it blocks a basic acknowledgement attached to the fact that the freedom of the human being is of a social nature. Most simply stated:

> The point is not to become free from other human beings, but to become free with and among them.[88]

This can also be expressed as follows:

> To be oneself, however, does not imply, as many seem to believe, that the single individual is less dependent on others. Human beings are social beings. The creation of one's own identity happens in meetings where others confirm the choices one makes, and each individual needs these meetings in order to see the validity of the values one expresses as important. [89]

---

[88] James (p. 10).
[89] From a chronicle by Britt Kramvig in the Norwegian newspaper *Bergens Tidende*, 18th December 1999. My translation from Norwegian.

Our common sense morality is stuck with the language that rules in the communities where we develop our identities and our strong value standards – where what matters most deeply is to be seen and recognized by others as whole human beings. The fight over the moral language in business life is therefore obviously a fight over the quality of the business climate, and at the same time a fight over our possibilities of realizing deeper values in business life. "The fight for market power" can also be seen as a metaphoric hold in a fight that is just as much about the power of defining concepts as it is about market shares – a fight that easily ends with a constriction of our understanding of economic reality. For the individual as a subject of meaning creation in business life, this kind of metaphor might correspond badly to its pluralistic self-understanding, and at the same time restrict the possibilities of finding belonging and realizing good, virtuous relations to others.

## Moral responsibility and self-respect

In the middle of this it is important to be able to see that the individual-in-the-company does not exclusively take up a formal position or a readily defined role in a community. Why is this an important point? It is important because it is only from an external point of view (just as insensitive to human self-understanding as the nominalistic economy perspective) – that is, from a theoretical and reifying position – we can claim that organisations can act, have identities, that organisations are responsible and have their own agendas. Even if the individual is matured to responsibility within communities, it is always, as it unfolds seen from the inside – from a social actor's perspective – the single individual that sets goals, that brings responsibility into the company through making choices and, by acting, interprets reality and formulates its interpretations into an internal agenda. *It is only the single human being, with its conscience, that can be a moral, interpreting subject.* The moral responsibility must always be managed by individuals with courage and personal, as well as professional, integrity.

But companies can of course be more or less responsible. They can even be considered the central acting parties in a global play for money, power and good reputation. This therefore seems to be all about our choice of description level. Large corporations shape society more than ever, both directly and indirectly through such things as lobbying and influencing the media. But in this last point lie the limitations of such a description as well, if we, by responsible, mean *morally* responsible. Only persons can be morally responsible, since moral responsibility is attached to our personal identity. And identity is a normative concept, a concept that covers how persons orientate in a value-laden landscape and by that shape themselves in light of what they consider praiseworthy. Companies have a kind of identity, but this is a descriptive identity — they *are* their reputation, they *are* the way they are regarded, the idea the market and society has of them. Their identity is something they are attributed and that they live of or die from, while the normative identity that lies as a basis of moral responsibility is about an original will and expressivity.

From the view of each individual it is therefore always so that the contribution to company life is to be incorporated in a uniform and coherent story about one's own personal life. The single individual will always and inevitably worry about whether choices made in the service of the company will fit into the whole picture of oneself, a picture consisting of one's strong evaluations. Statements such as "the only moral obligation of a company is to make as much profit as possible", and a long list of other macho and market metaphors, are therefore only possible to make from an external viewpoint, a position defined entirely by rules in an impersonal system. It is morally unbearable for single individuals to say in principle "anything goes" in the service of the company.

By that we have approached something very fundamental seen from an inner, actor's perspective — a thought crucial to any virtue ethics: our self-respect is closely connected to the idea that there is an "I" that is to be maintained throughout all of the actions we conduct. We are supposed to be able to integrate them into our picture of what a good human life is. To say that we, in our roles in working life, should put aside our "personal moral opinions", is actually to say that we, at the end of the day, should stop caring about our self-respect. This is of course absurd. To put it in Aristotelian language: to succeed at work has to be a part of succeeding as a whole human being. In other words, as a virtue ethical position, Solomon's position is an important and much longed-for whole picture that can adjust the comprehension (by many) that business life can have its own ethics.

Business is not "just business" in itself, but is already from the beginning part of something larger, culturally, ecologically and morally. It is by the way possible to reach nearly the same conclusion if we see this from a liberal, ethical perspective of duty. We can express this in Kantian terms, namely as a safeguard of the autonomy of each single human being — that the idea of company fellowship can never deprive the single human being of its status as an independent and responsible, autonomous person. In order to keep one's self-respect, we must then say that one must be able to evaluate oneself from an impartial moral — and not role-defined — point of view. As the philosopher W. K. Frankena states:

> Self-respect is a conviction that one's character and life will be positively judged by any rational actor that evaluates it from a moral point of view.[90]

---

[90] Frankena (1973).

The personal responsibility for one's own life is inevitable; it is simply one of the most ineradicable elements of our modern ethical consciousness. This argument can however also be applied against Solomon's community project: maintaining self-respect implies that one is able to take responsibility for ethical problems that point beyond the company, or any form of community, problems that in their utmost instance can threaten the company's profitable activities or even its survival. Self-respect is attached to how "any rational actor" sees and judges one's actions. This states a responsibility, justified by appeal to a deep, freedom-constituting rationality, which expands beyond the company as a limited community.

Self-respect is attached to something else, something much more comprehensive and demanding than feeling complete in the company service as this at any time is defined by the company community – in organizational culture – itself. It must be remarked, though, that Solomon himself not by any means locks the individual moral responsibility into the company. His position is, quite to the contrary, partly an explicit confrontation with more extreme forms of communitarian ethics. For example he states: "…the nostalgic (I think purely imaginary) communities described or alluded to by recent virtue ethicists, often defined by a naïve religious solidarity and unrealistic expectation of communal consensus … Corporate cultures like the larger culture(s) are defined by their differences and disagreements as well as by any shared purpose."[91] Here we can see his conception of business ethics pointing in the direction of the open, dialogical organisation more than being tied to the idea of full-blown consensus-seeking corporate communities.

---

[91] Solomon (1997, p. 213).

## Community citizenship is not corporate citizenship

By that we are approaching a phenomenon that is given relatively much space in business ethics, namely what one now speaks of as "whistle-blowing". Blowing the whistle and alerting the outside world to ethical violations committed in company service, has in many ways been deemed personal responsibility par excellence in business life. In each case there is a story about how loyalty to the company yields to the individual's obligations to something more substantial. The phenomenon has to be seen consequently in light of the division between micro- and macro-ethical problems in business ethics, where one, among other things, states that any company internal loyalty norm has its moral limits. That it after all is a praxis internal norm that has to be accepted as praiseworthy in a wider perspective by each single responsible person. Loyalty is not moral until one has asked: loyalty to what?

This is of course not the same as saying that the individual will always be morally required or morally allowed to publish such information. Relatively strict criteria must be met: for example, that one has tried to discuss the case internally, and the fact that the management has given its blessing to the morally inexcusable actions has been brought to the attention of the board of directors. Moreover, more substantial criteria concerning the degree of seriousness have to be devised, and here we of course land in difficult, but in practice normal considerations that demand trained judgement.[92] It is of course not possible to give a general rule for where the limit has to

---

[92] This is normally formulated somewhat like this: the damage the discussed decision can cause has to be substantial and probable. In addition one usually demands that one has to possess information that will also convince others that the case is morally objectionable in an impartial evaluation, and possibly also a consequentialistic requirement that announcing the information will lead to preventing the damage, or at least will limit the consequences considerably.

be, because here we need the practical wisdom of each individual to step in and decide through conceptualising and interpreting the situation.

However, we can not go deeper into the practical and organisational aspects of this particular problematic here.[93] We will only note how alerting behaviour can be legitimised, namely by the sovereign responsibility of each individual to avoid contributing to doing bad. This independent of any established loyalty demands and economically funded community obligations. We can say that it is the normative dimension which discusses the individual duties and rights that here impinge on, or draw the limits of, a virtue ethics that focuses on the internal goods that can only be realised within the framework of a community.[94]

But we can also, of course, say that this shows how organisation and community are not the same thing, and that Solomon mixes these two different things together. The formal organisation, one can claim, is never the same as the communities formed and continuously reformed by the company's members. Once we make this distinction, we see that the relation between organizational values and individual responsibility is not simply about the individual's duty to adapt those ready-made values. To see oneself as a community member in working life is more about the internal values of real communities, communities built within the organisation, than sticking to – or departing from – common values underlying company goals. It is only such real communities that can be said to be their own goal – a real

---

[93] For an example, clarification and discussion of "whistle-blowing" see French (1995, part 2, chapter 8), Green (1994, chapter 4), and the first part of Bowers/Mitchell/Lewis (1999) for some important and notable examples on successful, unsuccessful and fatal lack of alert.

[94] Of course alerting can in some cases also be legitimised both virtue ethically (in a virtue ethics that not so strictly attaches the virtues to the internal goods of given communities, but more generally to the question: what kind of human being do I want to be – and how do I keep my soul through these actions?) and consequentialistically (one calculates that the best total result will follow from announcing the information).

Aristotelian praxis. And it can also be claimed that attempts at defining company values, especially if one confuses them with the development of real communities, can create just as much alienation and disintegration — rather than healthy socialisation — as the widespread use of economic incentives. As asserted by Lars Klemsdal: "Good, inclusive work communities can only be achieved as a by-product of good organisation and never as a secondary goal in a principal organisational strategy."[95]

A community-focused virtue ethics will, not surprisingly, consequently not fill the whole ethical picture in business life. At least if we do not separate the community of interacting individuals from the defined organisation and its official values. One definitely important matter is sensitivity to what role the community has for the refinement of the individual. Another just as important ethical dimension is preventing evil actions committed in the service of the community (or rather, the organisation). Our ethical sensitivity therefore has to create space for a concept of actions that we, free of exceptions, should not do, contribute to doing or accept as done by others if we know they are about to happen. Given, among others, the Kantian acknowledgement of the significance of ensuring the humanity in both oneself and other persons, we can reasonably claim that we are more clearly obligated to not do evil than we are obliged to promote good. To avoid cruelty and harm can, as we saw in Chapter 2, be made the core of liberalism.

Any acceptable business ethics therefore seems to have to include both strong Aristotelian and Kantian elements, in addition to the utilitarian dimension that defines the basis of the calculation of economic value. Personal integrity is in other words a virtue that balances between conformity and (sometimes hard-won) independence: a balance between adjusting, finding the harmony of the community,

---

[95] Klemsdal (2004, p. 137). My translation from Norwegian.

and being able to correct the course of the community from an impartial moral point of view. Integrity is closely related to being able to feel *complete*, but this feeling of being complete must not be mistaken with the feeling of social comfort and convenience. Good employees are good people. And one is not a good person solely in the strength of being a good employee, by holding professional integrity. Personal integrity therefore assumes courage. Courage and personal integrity are in other words moral virtues that are very closely connected.

The company as an organic unity can undoubtedly create and maintain a real union between human beings, with great impact on both moral sensitivity and courage. That the company could be a common praxis with common goals in which the single individual could find security and meaning is still, though, an idea of something of which we should be critical. Putting too strong a focus on the positive "internal moral life" of the company can displace the necessary moral focus on the company's superior legitimacy in society, and likewise cover up the powerful ideological elements that give such legitimacy. We have therefore brought the idea of corporate citizenship too far if we accept it as a dominant part of our citizenship. The single individual's citizenship is never an "indirect society citizenship" through corporate citizenship. We do not want closer and stronger company communities as an answer to what many claim is the crisis of meaning in our late modern society. Not if this at the same time locks us out of being able to raise our responsible voices as individuals.

## Profit and a mechanical view of the human being

We stated earlier that the concept of corporate citizenship does not only deal with the relationship between individuals and the company as a community, but also the company's role as an actor in relation to its surroundings, its environment in an extended sense – to the society as a whole and the local community in particular. The basic idea here is that companies and their activities have to be seen as an integral part of the body of society, and not as juridical or economically limited units in it. The same holism that manifests itself when we observe the relationship between the individual and the company (or at least the real communities within it) will by far be manifested when we observe the relationship between companies and society. In the same way that our professional role in working life can not be isolated from life as a whole, the company can not be isolated from society as a whole. In our perspective here, companies are an integral part of society by virtue of their power and resources that are included in our conception of social development.

Any social phenomenon is what it is by virtue of its relations to something else. And the most obvious relation here is that all business activity, all economic means, to the utmost serves personal consumption. Company life without consumer life simply makes no sense. The main point is always whether economic activity results in *valuable consumption*, and seen thus, consumption is undoubtedly not only the economical but also one of the moral foundations of business life. It is not therefore concluded that the values realised by consumption should be the only source of moral consideration in business life, but in this lies the notion that economic activity can not be exclusively legitimised in any other way either. A market economy with free producer and consumer choices is a natural extension of our understanding of liberal society, where making one's own decisions is assigned independent, inherent value. We must remember that, basically, money is nothing else or more than what any group of human beings decides to use as a medium of exchange. Profit understood as an amount of money is therefore not a particularly interesting matter. What the profit symbolises is however deeply interesting, and it is at this point that consumer life is directly actualised as part of any business ethical perspective:

Profits ... symbolize what people want, and what people are willing to pay for what they want... Clearly, then, profit represents human achievement and social good. It symbolizes the contribution of business to communal and personal well-being.[96]

Understood in accordance with (neo)classical economic thinking it is relatively uncomplicated to furthermore see the connection between consumption and an increase in welfare and social prosperity. In such a perspective a product is defined exactly as a bundle of functional qualities, and consumption is presumed to be structured by these actual qualities of the product. These qualities give advantages and utility by contributing to the solving of concrete problems in everyday life. A rational match between the problem recognition of the consumer and the product qualities will in other words mean growth in private wealth. If we in addition add corrections for so-called third party effects, for example in the shape of taxes (that actually can be said to change the active causal chains of economy), we come even closer to a simple correlation between consumption and wealth on an aggregated society level as well.

So what is the point in presenting such a simple socio-economic consideration in this context? It is this: as we also pointed out in Chapter I, under the assumption of so-called perfect competition, it can be claimed that each company's social responsibility corresponds perfectly to its economic responsibility. We remember Milton Friedman's contention that a company only should maximise its praxis internal goals in the market. But – and here we are getting close to the genuinely ethical point – we do not see this in the same way as a *natural* standing if we, from the very beginning, see the company as a genuine human community constructed around whole meaning-seeking human beings that continuously question their values. And

---

[96] Primeaux (1997, p. 316).

not least, if we see the company as a responsible community in a larger society from which it obtains its different resources and also significantly influences culturally.

## Corporate social responsibility – an extended value consciousness

The diversity of resources that a company obtains from its surroundings, the diversity in the interests that legitimately follow these resources, and, not least, the diverse ways in which the company by its economically charged reality comprehension influences society – it all points in the direction of a demand for an extended value consciousness. And with that, an extended concept of social and moral responsibility. In a philosophical perspective it is natural to attach this concept of extended social responsibility to the fact that we have different levels of ethical evaluation, and by that, different types of objects of responsibility also. Examples of ideal-types of such moral objects range from one's self (to keep one's self-respect), via the concrete Other (ethics of closeness), to future generations (the impetus for wise decisions and everybody's right to cover their demands) and animals, plants and eco-systems (according to deep ecological thinking).

In a company perspective it is, however, based on the assumed underlying economic norm of reciprocity (mutuality, balanced terms of trade), normal to approach the ethical responsibility objects indirectly through a concept of legitimate, stakeholder interests. According to this model the company is to be considered as a collection of groups where the goal is, precisely, to preserve the equilibrium of the organisation. In this model one therefore analyses the contributions to and from the company related to different stakeholders, such as lenders, employees, owners, customers, suppliers, labour organisations, different parts of the public sector, among others. It is, however, a central question if such a stakeholder model actually breaks with a mechanical and value monistic understanding of economic value creation.

A stakeholder way of thinking can relatively easily be anchored in Solomon's communal approach to the company, which he also states in the following, commenting on the necessity of extending the responsibility perspective from the unilateral profit interest of the shareholders, the so-called owners of companies:

> The central concept in ethics for business life is the idea of social responsibility ... It is a concept that has annoyed many adherents of the free market ... All that carry the company shall benefit from the social responsibility of the company, the stock holders are just one small sub group. Those who carry the company are all that are affected and have legitimate expectations and rights related to the company's activities. That is all employees, the consumers, the suppliers and the whole society.[97]

Solomon obviously means that Friedman is wrong, that he has got it all upside down. Managers in business life are not only the shareholders' "trusted agents with a trusted responsibility" to unilaterally increase the profit. Managers are placed in the middle of a web of different interests and claims, and their responsibility therefore has to be seen from several points of view. The extended value consciousness is no *burden* for the company and its management; it should be seen as an essential and from the very beginning integrated part of the company's task. Still, as a measure of moral responsibility in company life the stakeholder model has its definite limitations, even if the model represents a healthy extension of the perspective related to the focus on the shareholders' economic claims alone. And the

---

[97] Solomon (1992, p. 19).

critical point is the underlying norm of reciprocity. As shown in Chapter 3, not all parts of our moral consciousness can be captured in concepts of balanced yield, just reciprocity and stable organising and management of given interests. Not all of the company responsibility can be defined within a contractual framework. It is therefore not unproblematic when we try to incorporate the company's extended social and moral responsibility into such an interest-based model.

It has great appeal, though. And we can find an operationalisation of the company's extended social responsibility along these lines in what is called ethical accounting. That the idea behind ethical accounting builds on a stakeholder model, and thus is encumbered with its weaknesses, should be obvious in the following concept clarification stated by one of the originators of ethical accounting: "Ethics as ... a set of values between an organisation and its stakeholders, that expresses which claims will apply for the decisions of the organisation."[98] Arne Johan Vetlesen comments on this idea, that social and moral ties are the origin of social and moral obligations only when they come out of "free choices" made by autonomous individuals, with the following statement: "The model is philosophically attractive, but its content completely misleading. What is wrong? To comment on this in a communitarian way, we can say that the description of social and moral relations as some kind of 'contract' is incorrect in itself. As soon as we are requested to think in the terms of a contract, we are brought, not closer to the core of moral obligations, but further away from it."[99]

The idea of reciprocity can sometimes stand in opposition to our moral obligations. The Kantian duty is, as we have seen, distinctly *not* interest-based. It touches on moral relations that exist independently

---

[98] Bak (1996, p. 31). My translation from Danish.
[99] Vetlesen (1996b, p. 19). My translation from Norwegian.

from the interests we or others might have as beings with needs and wants. That is: relations that are anchored in another kind of practical sense than the one that calculates and manages equal relations. By the way, the "anti-Kantian" moral sensitivity of the ethics of closeness also falls outside such reciprocity logic, because of its focus on demanding claims ahead of any form of economic calculations. Besides, the moral considerations that may come forward related, for example, to different environmental problems are directed straight towards "silent interest", and our considerations will therefore be rather artificial and not particularly identity-sensitive if they are treated as something that in the end shall be "commercially" based and understood. If these interests in a deeper sense are to be equally balanced towards other interests from a way of thinking that is commercially correct, they will easily come forward in pseudo considerations, such as this:

> Johansen underlines that DnB's environmental strategy is commercially based. For the credit operations it implies that the ethical and environmental relations will be emphasised where such conditions can be of importance to the value of our security, the customer's ability to pay his debts and/or our reputation.[100]

In other words, understood in this way, environmental issues will only matter where other interests, and maybe in particular the owner's required rate of return, are affected. If environmental issues are to be incorporated in the company's moral responsibility, it should obviously not happen within the framework of such a stakeholder model. If the moral responsibility towards nature and environment is

---

[100] Interview with Jan Johansen, responsible for the environmental follow up in the former DnB (a Norwegian bank). Published on DnB's homepage http://www.dnb.no, autumn 2001). My translation from Norwegian.

to be manifested, it has to be aimed directly towards the company decision-making, and not indirectly through a model of legitimate and goal-carried interests. We shall, in other words, remember that the categories of responsibility that moral philosophy sketches belongs to basic ethics, and thus is on this side of the dominant economic interpretation of moral and social responsibility as the balancing of interests. Consequently even the extended stakeholder model presents only one among several possible and desired perspectives on the concept of responsibility.

The concept of the human-being-in-the-company consists of the individual as a responsible and self-realising citizen in the company service, but also points in the direction of the company as a responsible institution in the societies where it operates. And we have seen how these two dimensions are attached to each other in the holistic virtue ethical view that forms the basis of the idea of corporate citizenship. At the same time we have seen that this idea in spite of all its rich sides has its moral limitations. This applies both on a macro level related to the stakeholder-based understanding of social responsibility, and the possible blindness to personal integrity and community or organisational criticism on a micro level. It is therefore an important asymmetry in the double definition of corporate citizenship as we have presented it here: the individual is not closed into the company in the same way as the company is "closed into" society and its natural environment. But this asymmetry can not legitimize a view of the relation between individual and company as an instrumental relation, or a view of the company as an economic abstraction without power to shape human beings and the social climate within which they live.

Chapter 5

# Is economic reality growing?
More on economic power

When analysing society from a power perspective, economic power is often understood as controlling the economic means.[101] This is of course a conclusive element in how society functions, understood both as how money and material goods are distributed and the fairness of mechanisms creating this distribution. (And we may make a similar analysis when it comes to cultural capital, how it is distributed and how this constitutes and consolidates social differences.) But the concept of power that most fundamentally sheds light on social responsibility, is power as it is attached to language and communication, to discourse – to how the ways we talk and think represent borders between what is interesting and not interesting, important and not important, and determine who is attributed competence to decide "what is actually going on" when economic questions are dis-

---

[101] During the writing of this chapter I became aware of the recently published book, *Markedets makt over sinnene (The Market's Power Over Our Minds)* by Bent S. Tranøy, which, coincidentally, discussed in a very good way some of the approaches that I wanted to discuss here; several of the sections in this chapter are therefore influenced by this book. The book is strongly recommended for Norwegian readers seeking an evaluation of the power, dispersion and effect of the market through discussion of a wide range of enlightening cases.

cussed. Here we will basically take a closer look at the discursive aspects of economic power, which, by the way, covers much the same as we previously in Chapter 2 referred to as symbolic power.

Just as important as who is sitting on the money, is the dispersion of thoughts and attitudes that make money important – as a relevant value measure in a continuously greater part of society. In short, we are talking here about what and who is attributed the power to shape – mentally and culturally – the reality within which we act. The Norwegian philosopher Gunnar Skirbekk stresses, on a general basis, the influence this kind of power has on our discussion of social questions:

> This is not an innocent question, because if a case is discussed within economic concepts, we will primarily see economic values and norms, and if we primarily use sociological concepts, we will primarily see sociological values and norms, etc. What is the case, and who it is that defines it, will then be an important question in practical discussions.[102]

When we categorise something as an "economic question" or an "economic value" we do not attach neutral tags. If we use economic concepts, this will automatically be to decide to view the case from one side, or focus on certain aspects, and thus reduce the complexity that characterises any human situation. Of course this complexity has to be reduced to enable us to act, but it is our responsibility to see that this can be done in many different ways. This can therefore also be referred to as definition power, and we understand that it is not only about defining words and expressions; far less innocently, it is about deciding how we are to approach a situation and thereby decide how it is to be judged and handled. Definition power is decid-

---

[102] Skirbekk (2005, p. 80). My translation from Norwegian.

ing what ought to be considered the essential attributes of a situation. We understand that this is power that can not easily be traced to single individuals or definite groups that exercise power consciously and goal-directedly – it is a form of collective power, one that shapes ideas and attitudes on a level more fundamental than the practical level where decisions are made and strategies defined.

One example is how living without paid employment is referred to and understood as being un-employed; that is, based on a lack of something considered normal and valuable, namely *a lack of paid work*, and thus also economically problematic, as a personal problem and an untapped resource, requiring strategic actions to handle and eliminate it. In Chapter 2 I introduced the idea that paid work is not necessarily what ties us to the social community and the centre of value creation in society. Seen in this way, being without work is not (only) negative: "un-employment". It is another area for expression of life, an area that might not circle around material goods. At least then it is *possible* to see it differently, more of a challenge to our normal way of thinking when it comes to lived life and value creation. It challenges the power, since, as Hesselbjerg states: "One can also say that companies possess power by the fact that their provision of work is presented as a definite good for society."[103] As we touched upon in Chapter 2, the negative influences of work on society, on our common condition for life, may be substantial. Besides, life with work as a natural centre – education with a job as the goal, a long working life, then a post-job period as a senior citizen – is not a given life structure. It is a powerful, dominant interpretation in our time and culture.

What we therefore need are value concepts that are not shaped by the fact that our world is already uncovered, more and more, as an economic reality. This can be said to be radical – in the sense that it

---

[103] Hesselbjerg (2001, p. 261). My translation from Danish.

goes *to the root* (from Latin, *radix*: root) of how we see ourselves as responsible human beings. But even if we, in this chapter, primarily discuss economic power in a discursive sense, it might first be worth mentioning more concrete shapes of such power – just to remind ourselves that market solutions will not always be as efficient, and therefore not necessarily as praiseworthy, as they seem, even when we discuss them in markets terms.

## The ugly face of power *in* the market sphere

As we pointed out already in Chapter I, traditional economic theory studies praxis based on idealised assumptions that make power, norms and language-based cooperation invisible. The Norwegian critic of market liberalism, Bent S. Tranøy, makes a twist on the well-known economic expression *perfect competition* and suggests that we instead call it "utopian competition" or, with a humorous touch, even better: "totally unrealistic but still theoretically interesting competition."[104] In markets with completely unrealistic but still theoretically interesting competition, there is no power – it is a model of economic cooperation where independent actors with readily shaped preferences meet one by one without any kind of commitment or deeper link between them. All information is practically free of costs and available to everybody, and the markets are open for free entry and free exit without impediments. When we here state that there is no power, it is in the sense that full equality exists in the relation between separate economic actors.

But in practice, markets are not always fair, nor always very efficient. Any economist should know this – at least this last – since different shapes of so-called market imperfection or market failure are things that have long occupied economic theoreticians. It might be

---

[104] Tranøy (2006, p. 43). My translation from Norwegian.

that markets are characterised by imperfect competition because of large fixed costs, the consumers' incomplete information, negative or positive consequences for third parties (so-called external effects), or that the goods actually are of a collective kind such that several can enjoy them as soon as they have been paid for. Then, as we know, society's resources are not utilised efficiently when managed by the market. Let us just point out further aspects of the theme market power.

The point, related to power and unfortunate use of power *in* the market, is that such imperfections are easily hidden. Actually, we have become so accustomed to many of them that we almost consider them to be normal phenomena. Some of them, and these are the ones most likely to gain media attention, benefit single persons, like executive managers of companies that through option contracts can double and triple their annual income. How are such agreements possible we may ask, even in a number of public companies, when we in many cases can uncover that the underlying share value of the relevant companies will fluctuate as a consequence of conditions that have little or nothing to do with decisions made by management? And furthermore, how is it possible in an era of social responsibility, when such an award structure gives little or no meaning if we do not accept a narrow, short term management of companies based solely on the stock market as desirable? Later, though, the same companies can claim to show themselves responsible by living up to laws or public demands on publishing information about such salary agreements. It remains obscured that such award systems are possible only when someone, single persons and networks, have seized much power – partly by succeeding in telling the public opinion about an international (working) market for top executives, and giving a picture of negotiations between independent parties.

Power in the market can be found everywhere, since the power-free market is only an idealised model. In practice most markets are characterised by unbalanced distribution of power, and we might therefore be inattentive when it comes to challenging it. In a number of the markets that meet the needs of every day life it can easily be observed that we have a strong concentration of power with a few, dominating chains. This applies in grocery trade (in Norway both on the producer and the retail side), bank and insurance services, clothing, engine fuel, sports equipment, telecommunications and electricity, air transport and hotel stays. This is power in relations that have grown out of the market economic system as its practical functioning evolves over time.

In a number of markets large corporations have the power to influence their own market conditions, through lobbying, control of information flow and through professional opinion-forming. Then we can no longer take for granted that the necessary other part of economic ethics, "the hand of politics" as it is understood in this ideology, is at the ready to secure fair rules and the common good. The consumer political participation has virtually no access to this level of resources, and is of course characterised by far weaker organisation. Social responsibility will therefore in many instances also include strengthening the consumer where we want the market to work in the best possible way.

Thus the lesson here is that market-internal relations can often be very unbalanced – it easily turns out to be the little man against the large bureaucracy, not only in the relation between citizen and state that market liberalists have always been absorbed by, but also the relation between consumer and company. We can further find a theoretical basis for this in, among other things, the turning of economic theory in the direction of behavioural economics.

## ... and some behavioural economics

As pointed out in Chapter I, by focusing on conditions related to our lives as consumers, we want to discover things that may influence our understanding of social responsibility. By taking the consumer's instead of the producer's perspective, we find a number of new elements that touch on economic power in the market. Even if this does not necessarily show that the responsibility of individual companies expands into the consumer sphere, it shows clearly that the ethical considerations we should make at the society level is about how the market works in practice rather than its completeness under idealised assumptions.

The relatively new branch of economic theory called behavioural economics shows why ethical considerations apply to the relation between buyer and seller. This is shown by, among other things, exploring the asymmetry in the information and the means of power that often characterises this relation. Deregulation of markets therefore often means profit on the sales side at the expense of the buyer. Behavioural economics has, by empirically studying how people actually make their choices, first and foremost shown that the traditional economical theory of the human being as a self-disciplined and goal-directed "economic man" is highly unrealistic. We simply do not make our decisions as logical, rational and ultimately self-interested beings. We do not as a rule weigh costs against advantages and maximise total value and profit for ourselves.

A number of behavioural and cognitive limitations apply to our economic choices: we let ourselves be governed by the emotions of the moment, and by immediate gratification. We often do not have the self-discipline to follow our rational goals and ideals; we let the framing of alternatives shape our attitudes towards risk; we miscalculate probabilities; we save little when we should have saved much, and value money we already have more than the possibility of an equivalent profit; we let big, personal economic questions be influenced by small, aesthetical means in advertising. Furthermore, we say no thanks to free profit if we feel unfairly treated in a situation where profit is given; we perceive information that confirms our prejudices to be relatively more credible than information that tells us the opposite, leave more money at the restaurant if we like the background music, readily buy the more expensive item of merchandise if it is introduced as an alternative. And we let salesmen seduce us for the sake of the seduction. And the social consequences of this are large, not because it means we are foolish and must learn to be more rational[105], but because it means that the free market with perfect competition does not guarantee Pareto-optimal solutions.[106]

The deregulation of economic activity therefore does not need to be a step in the direction of the best possible welfare result. Seen in the light of the growing difference between well-educated and less or uneducated parts of the population that we find in a number of countries, behavioural economics rouses our attention to the allocation effect of deregulation and privatisation of markets. Relatively less knowledgeable, naive and moment-oriented people, risk loosing in a system where the counterparts are large corporations with major resources for influencing consumer interest and knowledge about influencing the consumers' framing of goods and services.

The problem can be said to be general, however, since it applies to us all that the time we have available for making choices in the market is limited. To create continuously new choice situations will not necessarily increase welfare, since both our will and ability to make good enlightened choices is limited. As stated by Tranøy: "Too many choices make us stop choosing, and thus choice becomes an illusion.

---

[105] When the findings of behavioural economics are presented as deviations from mainstream economics (that is assuming, more or less, the economic man as an ideal figure), it can quite easily be understood as a kind of foolishness. To avoid this one has to see such findings, not in the light of some fixed ideal, but as expressions of meaning that need to be understood with respect to other premises.

[106] A relatively brief and good description of behavioural economics, with concrete examples of its political influence, can be found in the article "The Marketplace for Perceptions", by Craig Lambert, in *Harvard Magazine*. The article can be found at: http://www.harvardmagazine.com/on-line/030640.html

Freedom of choice can seem to be – and is sold to be – an empowerment of the consumer, but in reality it implies a transfer of power to the large corporations."[107] In recent years we have had a deregulation of, among others, telecommunication and the electricity market, but indications are that most of us still end up using one of the large suppliers, those who are simply there when we do not have the energy to make our own, independent market choices. And then these suppliers can of course exploit their position, in our time squeeze and excess of choices, and price their goods accordingly. Most people have a life to live outside all markets, outside the consumer role, and choosing away has evident power consequences in the constantly emerging markets.

We stated above that in the model of the ideal market, power is absent. But it is still evident that the model itself has power. It provides, as stated, the picture of a "perfect" competition, an economy where free choices of goods are the ideal and social welfare is optimised as a consequence of the fact that each individual follows his/her isolated self-interest. It has definitional power, power to shape our comprehension of normal economical behaviour – and to shape our picture of the human being as such. In short it has the power to set the agenda, to make social aspects of society with substantial cultural and moral significance appear as deviations from, additions to or obstacles to natural, free, economic action.

## The power to shape our view of human nature

It is difficult to search for power in the depth of a theory that shapes dominant decision-makers' ways of thinking and has also got a good grip on people's self-understanding. To trace the concrete lines that go from theory to practice is of course an impossible task. Besides,

---

[107] Tranøy (2006, p. 205–206). My translation from Norwegian.

professionals often hide behind such statements as: theories "are only analytical tools"; "they only give partial pictures of behaviour" or "are not meant to describe the reality, but merely give a basis for prediction, for qualified guesses". But quite often something more attaches to our practical consciousness, and it seems reasonable to presume that the view – and the public discussions – will be increasingly shaped by the silent assumptions of economic theories. Besides, more than a few professionals would claim that there is much realism in these models, that economic theory actually carries with it insight into human nature itself: selfish, or at least self-centred, calculating and goal-oriented.

To challenge economists (and ourselves as such), we therefore have to be willing to move into other theoretical universes, for instance within anthropology or sociology – where we can find theories that try to repudiate that human beings fundamentally, or "actually", are such economic actors. Theories that claim we are meaning-creative in a number of ways and accordingly pull reality close to us also as genuinely non-economic practical reality. It is difficult but necessary to challenge the grip on our thinking that has been established by the economic view of the human being. In order to analyse discursive power and hegemonic thinking, it is necessary to be able to think that it is possible that capitalism, pure exchange relations and life dominated by activities in a money-based economy are not the answer to the true nature of human beings. That these phenomena should be considered more as historical forces which themselves have contributed considerably to the creation of the atomistic and instrumental picture of the human.

Here it is worth mentioning one of the dominant views on the growth of capitalism – in other words the growth of the market characterised by free competition as we know it from the economic reality of our time. This view, also called "the commercialization model", is based on the assumption that from the very beginning there exists a human "basic behaviour" that lies dormant and waits to find its outlet in free market capitalistic forms. The model is therefore connected to the modern idea of the human being as basically covetous that we sketched in Chapter I. What this model tries to tell is that capitalism grew as a *natural extension* of simpler forms of production and trade that have always existed. Capitalism was an inevitable (end)stage of development for the market when old barriers to free trade slowly, but certainly, were abolished in parts of Europe at the end of and just after the Middle Ages.

The history of the growth of capitalism is in other words the history of the final liberation of rational actors that through *all times have populated the market*. According to such a model all societies with markets are unreleased market societies. The American historian Ellen M. Wood puts it like this:

> The most common way of explaining the origin of capitalism is to presuppose that its development is the natural outcome of human practices almost as old as the species itself, which required only the removal of external obstacles that hindered its realization ... In these accounts, capitalism represents not so much a qualitative break from earlier forms as a massive quantitative increase.[108]

Capitalistic market forces are obviously strong forces. One can rather easily believe that the market is such an obvious and self-adjusting system, a system that is always close to optimal balance, some kind of harmony that arises almost per definition from the universal rational powers that exist. Liberalisation – that is, deregulation – of markets can therefore easily be grounded in such a universal picture of the

---

[108] Wood (1999, p. 11–12). For a brief and simple introduction to this view of the growth of capitalism (and some possible alternatives), see Part I of Wood (1999).

human being. But as Aasland states, there is something basically wrong in such a way of arguing, because again we find ourselves in a circle:

> But the theory of market balance is tautological. Since consumer preferences can not be uncovered in other ways than through observed choices, any situation can be described as optimal for the participants ... everything is solved, and there is nothing more to do. The system turns back into itself and reasons itself; it never exceeds itself ... the result is insusceptible to criticism because the solution "is simply there", and can always be explained as a balance between counteracting forces, much in the same way as for instance the weather.[109]

That things are "marked decided" does not automatically imply that things are as they should be – it does not display a "real economic world" behind the reality that is created as a result of our practical, and potentially value- and system-critical, choices. The forces that decide the weather are beyond us, while the forces that decide market solutions stand in an internal relation to ourselves. To say that there exists a market for everything is therefore just the same as saying that a price – and a produced amount – can be established for almost everything. But this does not mean there should be. As a part of our practical world, a price is never *automatically* a value seen in a social perspective, and never *completely* described as a result of balanced trade between covetous parties. In other words, prices are expressions of what and how we *actually value* things, but not automatically what and how we find things praiseworthy.

We can therefore rightly ask how liberal the market thinking often referred to as new liberal economic thinking actually is. When

---
[109] Aasland (1999, p. 17).

we speak of liberalisation today we often mean, as a basic rule, privatisation and the deregulation of markets. We do not mean protection of the individual's basic rights, strengthening of the citizen's democratic disposition, authorization of the single individual, or that the individual's refinement to freedom is a core social issue – that we need to secure institutional and value plurality in order to secure as much life space and authentic fundamentals of experience for the whole human being as possible. What one usually wants with liberalisation is to secure *maximum* freedom of choice for each individual, not to define *important, enlightened and meaningful* freedom of choice. It is therefore a specific economic power that makes liberalisation in our time mean free market and not the protection of diversity of (social) life. The picture of the human being that one builds is leaner than implied by most liberal political theories.

Philosophically, it is nothing but a misunderstanding that liberalism means atomism, that liberal thinking as such puts the individual first and downplays or neglects the influence of the society on individuals' development. We can, for instance, turn to the basic idea in the American philosopher George Herbert Mead's social philosophy that says that the isolated (atomistic) individual is a myth – an individualism based on an atomistic society model is quite simply invalid. The individual will always stand out from the group, and the development of consciousness therefore presupposes a complex web of social interaction. Such a basic idea is developed by, among others, the Canadian philosopher Charles Taylor, who sees the human being as an active self-interpreting individual which consequently needs access to a number of collective resources in order to create its self and personality. It is in this connection also worth mentioning that the more community-oriented models of society – often referred to as socialistic production and distribution solutions in economy – can be very well reasoned in an equality-oriented liberal theory (so-called egalitarian liberalism). To spread market solutions based on the idea of a simple autonomy, the idea that it will always be right to increase the amount of choice, is therefore not automatically reasonable according to liberal thinking.

As Taylor has pointed out, there is something rather suspect about any liberalism that puts free choice at the centre of our thinking of individuality, without at the same time discussing in which connections it will be *important* to make one's own choices. This creates a powerful argument against the idea that securing maximal freedom of choice, in a market sense of negative freedom (freedom from public constraints), should be a superior goal. A purely quantitative concept of freedom has paradoxical consequences, for instance the idea that a minimum of obstacles in traffic makes a society where one lacks any political and religious freedom more free than a society where traffic is strictly regulated, but one has political and religious freedom. This is exactly where the importance of freedom, tradition and a critical public life enables us as collective, communicating citizens to separate important from unimportant, distinguishing between the more and the less meaningful arenas for choice and expression, and thereby providing the basis for positive, authorized freedom. Mature, responsible persons are, as Gunnar Skirbekk also states, "not a natural phenomenon, which is quite simply there"[110]. Protecting personal autonomy – our ability to reflect and make enlightened decisions – demands restrictions on any form of power that can impair it. Autonomy, maturity and responsibility are thus not things we can simply presuppose in order to make economic theory complete.

Actors without social bonds and belonging within a social structure will not be able to act rationally in any distinct human sense. It is therefore far from unproblematic to claim that liberalism means that social relations are to be considered as contracts between independent and self-sufficient single individuals. If this is taken for given, we loose the possibility of seeing social life as that which

---

[110] Skirbekk (2005, p. 83). My translation from Norwegian.

makes rational individual life possible. We are unable ourselves to see what gives shape to self-interest and what makes efficiency and economic rationality matter. These social ways of thinking about individuality are all ways of thinking that belong to modern liberal philosophy, but that still easily end in an intellectual deadlock in the practical debate on the functioning of the market.

The model of the economic actor can in other words be no more than a sub-perspective of human action. If we want to understand the ethical and complete character of social responsibility, we need to challenge this narrow view of human nature. By taking economic exchange relations as a model for social relations in general, we cover up both what is going on in the actor's life and in the civil society. By doing so we cover up the substantial sources we have for being able to take responsibility, to shape alternative understandings of economic problems and to develop alternative ways of structuring economic action.

## Preferences, power and communication

One of the major problems with standard economic theory is the assumption of stable and *given* preferences.[111] The picture created is that we arrive at the market with readily prepared wishes and goals.

---

[111] That is: of a given, stable and consistent preference-structure. The preference concept is one of the concepts that have been given such a substantial place in economic theory that they do not seem to need any clarifying definition. They appear to be self-evident. In most standard textbooks on economic theory, the concept is considered having an obvious meaning, as here (Varian 1992, p. 94): *"When we write x>=y, we mean the consumer thinks that the bundle x is at least as good as the bundle y".* And that is it. But the expression "as good as" in this definition is of course radically understated as a practical concept. Possibly the clearest expression of the supposedly obvious in the preference concept can be found in Gravelle/Rees (1992, p. 68): *"The meaning of the terms 'preference' and 'indifference' is taken as understood; we take it for granted that everyone knows what is meant by the statement 'I prefer this to that', or, 'I am indifferent between this and (that'."*) Do we automatically know? How do we for instance know if the preferences are the individual's own, if they are authentic expressions of self-interest, the result of independent thinking?

As we have just seen, it is a major theoretical problem that this is not empirically correct — a number of the wishes, interests, frames of thinking and goals which determine our actions are shaped by relations *in* the market. It is a banal acknowledgement for any marketer — and strictly speaking a part of common sense — that it is inappropriate to talk about given needs, and far more interesting to discuss shapeable wishes, habits, lusts and action impulses.

A somewhat different, but still obvious problem is even more interesting seen from a philosophical point of view: if market solutions are to be promoted in continuously new and more social arenas, then, we have to ask, where are the wishes and goals that the market presupposes and is expected to meet supposed to be shaped and evaluated? If the most efficient solutions follow from our acting as consumers in an increasing number of contexts, where and how are we supposed to be able to secure that the efficient prosperity we have gained access to really corresponds to what we want as enlightened and rational beings? What we here catch sight of is that unless society secures the individual's access to arenas for education, refinement of interests and human growth, market efficiency is a value that is in danger of undermining itself through being emptied of meaningful content. This is both a traditional and rather obvious line of criticism, but it is easily forgotten in the eagerness of increasing efficiency and the rationalising (in a narrow sense) piece by piece of the body of society.

The American philosopher, John Searle, gives the following simple objection to preference-based economic theory: most of the cases of practical evaluation imply balancing inconsistent wishes, wishes that are in mutual conflict; and in addition our wishes often collide with other reasons for action, such as commitments, social norms and moral ideals. This ends in the following critical eye on the fact that economic theory chooses to describe rational action by presupposing that actors are equipped with a consistent set of preferences, and thus it disregards our actual and complex web of reasons for action:

> The problem with that answer is that in real life deliberation is largely about forming a set of preferences. A well-ordered set of preferences is typically the *result* of successful deliberation, and not its *precondition*.[112]

By showing the market's excellence through talking about preferences, one thereby, strictly speaking, presupposes what one is supposed to show. The critique is therefore based on the fact that a preference-based theory is far from the realities of our economic evaluations ("real life deliberation"). Thus it is also poor when it comes to capturing the most basic economic power relations – those which touch how we shape our preferences; our ideals, interests and goals in real life. The theory is simply silent when it comes to how this happens, it does not question if it happens in ways that individuals are conscious of and reflect about, or if it happens as a part of how power works. How dominant ways of thinking can be thought to shape people's everyday consciousness also remains beyond the scope of the theory as long as it does not reveal anything about the formation of preferences. Why people's preferences are in motion and change as a part of the conditions in normal, social everyday life is therefore a question we need to turn to other scientific theories and models in order to understand.

In the theoretical universe we are discussing here, it is not easy to talk about social life at all. Here we are all "social atoms" that live and make choices without really *relating* to each other. For instance, it is not possible to see from this theory that we can listen to what others have to say because it may be *valid*, perhaps morally valid, for ourselves. According to this theory we can at most influence each other's choices by taking

---

[112] Searle (2001, p. 30–31).

part in each other's utility functions. We can be sensitive to other people's welfare (which is determined, non-rationally and non-socially, by their preferences): your joy and benefit can please me, and therefore I can have as my preference that you should benefit from my actions. Or social norms are sanctioned by others so we include the danger of being punished by entering the wrong alternatives into our calculations. As soon as we introduce into the idea that we actually relate to each other through language, not from utility, but by wanting to gain different kinds of understanding, and are thus led by the strength of arguments, it all becomes much more complex – and far more real.

Jürgen Habermas is known as one of the theoreticians who has long championed another, fundamental approach to the inter-subjectivity that qualifies our actions. This, too, is an action theoretical construction, but a pluralistic position. In short, it says that our practical rationality can be confronted with three completely different situations, or more precisely: the question "What should I do?" has, accordingly, three different meanings and indicates three different situations of action: a) What is the most appropriate means for solving this problem/reaching this goal?, b) What actually are my basic values and goals?, and c) How shall we impartially decide what is just and solve value conflicts between human beings? These are the basic questions in, respectively, *pragmatic*, *ethical* and *moral* discourse. Questions (b) and (c) are not instrumental, not result-oriented, but genuinely oriented toward better understanding – something that implicates cooperation and argument above competition and negotiation. This is most clearly seen from the normative acting situations in (c), where to take an impartial standing is included as a completely vital element in acting rationally. Precisely because we are linguistic beings – and in Habermas' thinking we can not separate language and action, since language *is* (social) action – we are also rational by being subject to definite context-dependent validity claims.

The picture of the human being that follows from such a pluralistic concept of rational action is consequently not one of a lonely monologist that tries to maximise his utility or profit, but of several collaborating actors that coordinate their understanding and their plans through preceding communication. The goals are made problematic, not only the means for reaching them. Situations are attempted, understood and re-created collectively. A basic point here is that before we can make rational decisions, we must understand the situation in which the decision is to apply. A legal proceeding can, for instance, very well be studied as a strategic play between the prosecutor and the defender, a contractual negotiation as a play between buyer and seller and a family at a play between man and woman or parents and children. But neither legal proceedings, business cooperation nor family life can be established from instrumental considerations and decisions alone. First the different social situations have to be constructed symbolically – made real and action-demanding – through comprehension oriented co-action. Economic rationality can not, therefore, be rationality in its most basic form.

With a basis in such a position, an important step in the direction of economic social responsibility will be to create real arenas for dialogue between all involved parties, so that different understandings of what is at stake can come forward. Rational action requires rational understanding of the multiplicity of any situation. But this also requires maturity in the domain of philosophy of science: that we develop a somewhat humble attitude by recognizing our own perspective on things – that our points of view are powerful because they determine our understanding and our action-readiness.

## Perspectives and the revealing – and concealing – of reality

Let us now take one step backwards and take a closer look at what the basic philosophical statement is here. Because in most of what we have said so far about economic power lies a basic point in hermeneutical human science: that understanding implies an act of revealing facts, and that revealing is at the same time concealing – that, in other words, knowledge is always closely attached to ignorance. Operating with a conceptual and methodological system, or a perspective as we often call it, does not only imply that parts of reality are described and explained, but that at the same time something is also left out and maybe even distorted. As Gunnar Skirbekk states, it is, for instance, not "wrong to refer to the students as 'consumers of courses', but it is still not the most adequate conceptualisation of students and what they do at universities and colleges."[113] Our practical experiences, for instance in the case of studying, often resist being described with language and concepts that do not fit, that distort and limit our original meaning creation. The basic point is that it is therefore necessary, in order to prevent economisation from undermining the goods that we reflexively feel praiseworthy, to look for understanding of what it is in our lives that rejects economic conceptualisation. Or at least resists it being the dominant conceptualisation.

The word perspective indicates, however, that we are talking about something here that we more or less freely can *establish*, almost as if we, with binoculars, fix the view of a section of the scenery from a defined angle. But such a physical space-related metaphor works poorly here, since it presupposes some scenery in which we find ourselves. By *perspective* we in this connection mean neither a freely chosen method of observation nor a larger overview, but a dominant non-neutral approach composed of a defined set of concepts. This set of concepts shapes both research and political decisions by carrying within it a fundamental view of the human being and society – that is, it carries certain ontological ballast (some kind of silent agree-

---

[113] Skirbekk (2005, p. 106). My translation from Norwegian.

ment on which phenomena exist and are important). To acquire the knowledge of a theoretical discipline and thereby gain perspective is, to be precise, to acquire the world as an organised and structured reality.

In Martin Heidegger's philosophy, according to the Norwegian philosopher Rune F. Nicolaisen, it is indeed so, that "a statement only can be said to be true or false based on a horizon that is already uncovered."[114] We can, for instance, encounter nature as an object of study within, shall we say, biology, or we can be engaged with it in an economic approach as, for example, the owner of a timber forest. To claim that the whitewood forest has a life cycle of approximately 70 years is meaningful only in an economic sense, for the land owner in his economic perspective, and makes less sense for the biologist within his horizon of understanding. It is a truth that belongs to that kind of understanding or "manner of being related to" natural surroundings. The general point is: before we can talk about single truths, the world has to be interpreted and understood in a defined way – and as a rule the world can be understood in a number of ways, at least the social world we inhabit as economic actors. And herein lies the underlining of the ambiguousness and complexity of human matters.

From the view of philosophy of science, the challenge we face is that we never encounter a language-independent world. The situation is rather that we, in different social practices, create linguistic symbols and systems that afford us the possibility to grasp and handle parts of the world as real. Something conventional ahead of our empirical study of social reality will, therefore, always exist. Our (at least partly) unconscious perspective is involved in deciding *how the world is supposed to appear to us*, both as everyday people and as professionals. The power critical point in this is that it is always threatening

---

[114] Nicolaisen (2003, p. 165). My translation from Norwegian.

when one type of interpretation *becomes* our unique reality. The criticism of positivistic philosophy that has always had a strong position in economic science has had it basis here. In the aforementioned critiques of positivism by Hans Skjervheim, the core point specifically is the struggle with the idea of a pure, academic social science: one must always account for oneself, and include one's perspective shaped view in considering when scientific knowledge should be communicated and used. And what is distinct about human science is that one is studying self-interpreting subjects. Professionals have to relate to a subject of study that means something about itself and has is its own self-understanding.[115] It is therefore evident that contact with reality is established, not by catching independent facts, but through a scientific interpretation of something that already is loaded with meaning. And such material of meaning is always "heavy" – ambiguous, many-faceted and fragile – which makes the significance of scientific perspectives considerable.[116]

At the same time there are obvious examples that a cultivation of one perspective can quite easily twist a number of facts in such a way that we end up with regular misconceptions. One such example is the conception that value is created only in the private sector. It has almost become a saying that value is created in the private sector – that is: in the market – while in the public sector part of this value is used, and consequently, private business life is financing public enterprise. But by claiming this, one will, in an unfortunate way, mix value creation with the funding of activities. What determines the actual

---

[115] If not, one becomes a spectator rather than a participant, something that according to Skjervheim represents both a misunderstood objectivism in science and a morally challengeable approach to human beings. "Deltakar og tilskodar" ("Participant and Spectator") is also the title of his perhaps best known philosophical essay (printed in Skjervheim, 1996).
[116] Which also means that human sciences will inevitably consist of interpretations of interpretations (what is often called "double hermeneutics"), and in that way will always be a reinterpretation of meaning seen from the primary practice position.

creation of value must certainly be *what one produces* – and not *how it is funded*. Public colleges are not simply using portions of the money made (and paid in taxes) by private colleges. The value created is much the same, even though the funding is different. The error made here is in putting an equal sign between the fact that value is created and consumers' willingness to pay. Again we see how the power of the dominant economic discourse may manifest itself in our view of society.

Besides, this is not just a scientific or cognitive problem: if we put private sector = value creation and we in addition let this mean that public sector = consumption of resources, we have made it difficult to argue for certain social solutions to economic problems. It should therefore be obvious that a market economic perspective might put us on some wrong tracks, or that we, by purifying an economic perspective to some kind of economics-ism, will miss important management information that might arise via other perspectives.

## Counter power requires diversity in perspective

A somewhat different way of presenting the impact of this is to say that there will always be an epistemological intention or interest that is a basis for knowledge, for the "choice" of a knowledge producing perspective. The new-pragmatist Richard Rorty, with whom we became acquainted in Chapter 2, insists that the object is always shaped by the perspective (or by the vocabulary, in his usage). This breaks with the normal, intuitive picture of scientific research where we discover, rather than create and shape truths, but makes it at the same time easier to see the leading power that lies in the perspective.

Rorty further states that based on political and moral intentions it is correct to study the human being as if it *is* its "network of beliefs, desires and emotions with nothing behind it"[117] Just as the

---

[117] Rorty (1997, p. 332).

human being in ballistic studies *is* a mass point, or as in chemistry it *is* a connection of molecules, it will, in its life practice, merge into its contextual and socially based understanding of what it is doing. There is no core or essence within the human being that forces us to take a given perspective – and the human world is silent on how it *really* should be described, as well – which also means that we are not tied to certain system-defined practical solutions.

According to this pragmatism it is therefore not correct to say, for instance, that economists, by studying the changes in measurable prices, can prove that there actually *are* economic laws that govern development, independent of how human beings act and interpret themselves. Pragmatically, one should speak within an epistemological rather than an ontological horizon, and say that we are speaking of statistical regularities that occur under certain social and historical conditions and that *create* the idea of, just as much as they represent, economic laws. Knowledge is not put forward as a more or less correct picture of reality from our cognitive abilities, but as a tool for our need to adjust to or handle the reality in certain ways.

By using a certain scientific conceptualisation, things are consequently revealed and reality steps forward in a fixed – and thereby necessarily limited and limiting – way. This is how we can see moral norms both as something that we as rational beings are forced to explore the validity of, to acknowledge the normative power in and rationally feel directed by, or something that we follow only if breaking them involves too high a cost in proportion to a self-interest that is not normatively defined. Our awareness of the latter will, however, tend to be hidden when dominating scientific language flows into our daily language and becomes *the* general understanding of what things consist of and how things are connected. Just as, for instance, Freudian terminology is now ingrained as an integrated part of the everyday physiological language – and comes forth almost as a blueprint of how the human mind works – it can seem as though the market economic language has fastened its grip on "how we really make rational choices" and "how we can best organise value creation and the allocation of goods". Then moral norms and ethical ideals *become* something conditional and almost random, in the form of something relative and subjective, that we can relate and adapt to like any other aspect of our surroundings.

The remedy for the power of thought (so-called hegemonic ways of thinking) or discursive power is therefore obvious: perspective diversity. To possess counter-power is to know other ways of understanding the relevant issues. Under this lies a basic point of pragmatic philosophy: the only real protection against inauthentic reification of current principles of organisation and rationality is in developing a pragmatic understanding of social life as fragile, complex and unstable. We can not live of course without presupposing that a number of social phenomena have some degree of stability and duration. But it is crucially important to our social responsibility that we acknowledge that this is something that we presuppose because we, practically speaking, have to, and not because that's just how reality is. The social reality is something we construct and institutionalise, not something that finds its shape independent of how we interpret our ways of feeling and acting. Our action-driven self-understanding is liquid. As the British philosopher Simon Blackburn comments, to again relate to the academic world: "A generation ago, nobody would have predicted that reputable professors of philosophy would think of themselves as managers and their faculties as cost-centres."[118] What has now nearly become the natural way of understanding how to operate a university was not long ago both strange and undesirable.

In the same way, economists can, for instance, claim that it simply *is so* that production of electric power is a business activity just like

---

[118] Blackburn (2005, s. 101).

any other business, and on that basis reject subsidies of power to defined industries.[119] But of course this is not necessarily how it "is", even if deregulation and internationalisation of the power market at a certain time has made it relevant to discuss these matters this way. Power production and distribution can very well be seen and conceptualised in other ways, and the most obvious is as a part of the infrastructure of society, as a basis of common good – or a "natural monopoly", if we like – which is exactly what was the "natural" perspective in Norway up until the liberalisation of this market in the beginning of the 1990's. Nothing just *is* a business in itself. No economic realities hang in the air unaffected by our earthly practical adjustments and ideals. The public debate can not be grounded on assumptions that some of us are able to simply discover what is a matter of business.

## To comply with economic realities

A number of important value problems are pushed aside or at least in the distant background because we so easily point at the "economic realities", as if they were natural forces. This because we thereby are actually creating a dramatic impossibility of system criticism and management by values, even if we nevertheless try to make adjustments of society to "human nature" appear as an assurance of future prosperity for an increasing number of people through economic growth.

Jon Hellesnes writes, as shown in Chapter I, very concisely about this form of model power, that organising in systems leads to reification and a following pulverization of responsibility. He does this, as mentioned, by underlining that "the argument behind the market solutions is that we need to adapt rationally to what is already our reality".

---

[119] See the Norwegian debate on industry and subsidies of electric power in the Norwegian newspaper *Dagsavisen*, toward the end of June and the beginning of July 2006. The economists I refer to are the professors Jon Vislie and Steinar Strøm.

And further, on the consequences of the distribution of power:

> Those who benefit from the spread of this way of thinking are above all the trans-national, capitalistic entrepreneurs... In using "the globalisation" as a pressure lies the fact that it is not actually the capitalists themselves who compel drastic initiatives. No, it is the "globalisation"... They have created an illusion of the un-political politics, that is, a politics that is about giving up the attempts to lead, and instead being "realistic" and adjusting to the demands of reality itself, the logic of global markets.[120]

And in the following Danish criticism of economic rationality we discover an almost identical indication of the strong covert power — a criticism that also directly shows the relevance in our context of the absence of real value questions in public debate:

> Many politicians insist that we must talk about values, but few of them show any interest in a discussion of, not to mention a limitation of, the market rationale and the growth that in spite of many principal speeches appears as the dominant goal and means of politics. A common political will to make the country best possibly equipped, economically, for a future global competition, pulls the teeth out of any fundamental discussion of how society is arranged... Both wings seems to follow a market thinking where legal regulations and public resources to an increasing degree shall fill a service function by giving access to the right possibilities for competence training and the optimal growth-stimulators in other respects.[121]

---

[120] Hellesnes (2004, p. 142–143). My translation from Norwegian.
[121] Fenger-Grøn/Kristensen (2001, p. 32). My translation from Danish.

In other words, the power of economic language does make an increasing amount of the activities in other parts of the society obliged to legitimise their existence as contributors to economic activities and innovations. And the reality is that the teeth are pulled out slowly, not only from a discussion of basic values and goals, but also from the practical possibilities to realise any other, more collective arrangement of society in a growing number of countries. The considerable growth in the world economy in recent years has created large surpluses in the multi-national corporations that dominate world trade, at the same time as these same corporations pay continuously less taxes to the communities from which they grow, within which they operate, and of which they presuppose the existence.[122]

Approximately 60 % of world trade is now conducted internally in multi-national corporations, and it is the different forms of internal pricing and "strategic allocation of profit" within these corporations that by far explains the tax reductions. This is, in Hellesnes' words, a concrete effect of an ideological blackmailing that happens by the very fact of the reification of economic reality – where each single actor adjusts optimally given the way the world "actually is". We can in theory also find such concrete effects of power at a micro level, in public organisations.

## Continuous change and economic model-power

Statistics tell us that just in the last two years a larger share of the employees in the public sector than in the private sector have had to submit to processes of major change and organisational readjustment (approximately 45 % versus 30 % respectively). These are processes that not only threaten the working conditions of each individual, but

---

[122] A very good news article on this, "Skattegåten" (The Tax-puzzle), can be found in the Norwegian newspaper *Morgenbladet*, 21st April 2006.

often touch upon the foundation of the enterprise itself, something that again changes the employees' self-understanding and contributes to change in how public goods are perceived and evaluated. And it is reforms that have economic considerations as their source that dominate in our time – it is about getting more welfare from the (taxpayer's) money. Because at the root of all this eagerness to change, there usually lies a model of the free market, a model that above all is meant to show the advantages of the free market when it comes to efficiency. Adaptation and change is equivalent to modernisation – that again is often the same as privatisation and market imitation. And modernisation is perhaps economic rhetoric at its most powerful.

But it is definitively possible to attach some doubt to the efficiency of market solutions when the goods produced are something rather different from toothpaste and chicken wings, things like care for the elderly, schools and administration of proprietary rights. It is a good ethical mnemonic rule to first examine what kind of good we are discussing, find its distinctive character, and then prescribe the solution to how it should be produced, distributed and enjoyed. This is the ethics in the big life – value considerations that penetrate politics and shape our culture in general. Here I had actually planned to discuss the ethics in the little life – in daily work, in how we understand ourselves in our job practice. What does the increasing interference from major changes mean here? Can ethics find footing in something that is always moving? What role does individual morality play when the structures are continuously changing? I believe the answers will show that the little and the big life are very closely connected.

My main statement is that we too easily individualise the negative and use structures to explain the positive in organisational change-processes. And the market model is then deprived of value-based criticism. "Lack of willingness to change" on an individual level is then a hindrance to a structure-defined development that is almost given by nature – along a line that is often given by professional change managers, that is. When an adaptation process has gone well, it consequently turns out to "work" measured in accordance with the new market-resembling standards; it is a proof that the model is correct. If it turns out badly, or is struck by major negative effects, this is caused by bad follow-up from the employees and generally low working morale, perhaps in combination with a little too obliquely designed motivational instruments. (A clear parallel to "you have only yourself to thank" if one is unsuccessful in the market society, while the system itself, it is said, generates infinite possibilities for those who know how to make the most of it.) Failure is rarely explained by the fact that new ways of thinking may possibly not make any sense to those who are supposed to do the job. It is in other words rarely explained by the rather "unfashionable" word alienation, even if this actually might be a phenomenon of increasing influence in today's working life – and maybe not so much as a consequence of changes in work content and routines, but through the spread of an almost impenetrable and irrefutable language.

One can easily begin to feel alienated in the world when one's reality to an increasing extent is described by "buzz-words" like continuous innovation, market orientation, modernisation, knowledge management, globalisation, value management, life-long learning and technology-based renewal. Empty phrases seldom allow for reflection, dialogue and will to change. But consultants, advisers and professional change managers often do their work under the cover of such an almost impenetrable management rhetoric. This adaptation elite quickly adapts any fashion in the management area, arches a justifying market heaven over the solutions they offer and moves quickly to their next project. They seldom have to live with the full consequences of the new solutions themselves. And as Bent S. Tranøy states: "What the change prophets seldom achieve, is the creation of a penetrating analysis that shows that the actions they suggest follow directly from a description and analysis of what is new in the world surrounding their organisation."[123] Changes are seldom justified in concrete analyses of a situation, but more often in ideological convictions. For people in this sector the expression "the world is changing" is, to a great degree, a self-fulfilling slogan.

The view of the human being that lies behind this wave of change is by far anchored in the strictly speaking antiquated economic picture discussed earlier – where management of a kind of natural egoism is in the long run the only management possible. Things and processes are consequently supposed to be sliced up and quantified, awarded and controlled. Adaptation and change are in the end necessary in order to adjust organisations to human nature. As human nature is, it is almost a law of nature that market solutions have to gain increased space in society. What we also fail to see here, however, is that there is no human nature independent of time and space – and thus no naturally given systems either. We human beings interpret ourselves. Change in the light of a given ideal is therefore too simplified to be successful.

The speed of this new wave of organisational change can therefore snatch away some of the basis for our everyday meaning creation. To work more on time limited projects can, for instance, undermine much of the durability that makes us feel confident both professionally and socially and consequently hinders the development of our critical sense. The same results from being moved around every so often, either on the organisational map or geographically and socially. And ethics is, as we have seen, criticism – of the dominant ways of thinking. Ethics is challenging power. Or to put it differently: ethics comes together with the acknowledgement that we always have a choice, that there are always alternative perspectives and ways of organising.

These are therefore conditions that we normally would say

---

[123] Tranøy (2006, p. 163). My translation from Norwegian.

impinge upon our ethical consciousness. In our daily practice ethics is dependent on a certain degree of slowness and long-term thinking. In the academic world – in higher education – development of a discipline is about establishing education and a research-based basis for perspectives that may take years to acquire. Integrity in the job then has to mean that one has the necessary tranquillity – and that one knows and accepts that it is all happening in a perspective of at least, say, five to ten years. Letting the development of courses follow the "trends in the market of educational services" in reality means that academic and professional development will become something other than it is today. Something other and *inferior* seen from within the academic tradition that one originally was to administer. Ethical awareness is then, based on our perception of how basic values change and make a liberal society poorer independent of any economic efficiency improvement. It consists here in being able to criticise the transition from student to customer and from professor to supplier of attractive packages of knowledge.

This situation counts for a number of public services – they have a value-based uniqueness that often fits badly with a market model where the legitimacy of decisions in the end comes from the user's experiences and willingness to pay. One therefore often has to fight hard to make the idealized model fit the value creation of human practice. And then we are at the core of my point here: if the structures are not adjusted to the properties of goods that are to be administered, it becomes artificial and very unfortunate to let ethics be about the working morality of each individual. High ethical consciousness is not only about the single individual and his/her moral decency within structures, but also *about the structures* each individual operates within. It is unreasonable to burden the individual with the weight of continuous changes – by explaining unfortunate deviations and consequences with individual factors – if these changes are a part of re-conceptualising and undermining the goods one is supposed to feel committed to creating. In our individualistic time we easily forget that ethics is not only a question of attitudes and character, but is also tied to the possibilities of system criticism, and that sensibility to value pluralism is an absolute condition for good ethical analysis of any modern society:

> A modern society needs a diversity of institutions and organisational forms, adjusted to different tasks ... The spectrum of organisational forms has to be broad in order to take care of the uniqueness of the different areas. This is precisely what the new liberalists do not see and do not want to see. They are victims of the illusion that a business economical model will fit everywhere.[124]

In the market ideology one often looses the view of the comprehensiveness of and diversity in the value creation made by the human being. At the bottom of this rhetoric of change and belief in business economic models, there lies an understanding of private money as good and pure money and, as mentioned, that "the public" only uses money. Pursuing the private (private initiative and innovation, private property, private business) easily goes together with scepticism towards anything public, neglecting that the private both presupposes and in multi-facetted ways works together with a well-functioning public sector. In a world that in many ways appreciates diversity and tolerance, it may seem as though just the opposite is manifested when it comes to organising and management principles. Here the economisation (read: new public management) has gained something close to monopoly. It is hard to argue against the "need to get more welfare out of the money", if one already in principle finds oneself within an economic interpretation frame.

In the age of continuous change, ethics should be about develop-

---

[124] Hellesnes (2004, p. 133). My translation from Norwegian.

ing resistance towards change for the sake of change alone and cut through the veil of fog that often characterizes talk of modernisation. It is about being able, through reflection and dialogue, to separate the good, really resource-saving changes from those which threaten to ruin values that are basic in a truly liberal, democratic development of the society. Ethics and social responsibility are therefore not so much about individual violations, as they are about sensitivity to social and cultural infrastructure in a broad sense – important virtues in the public, such as equality, empathy, open discussion, justice and refinement to maturity.

## When power is transferred to the individual

In the late modern work and everyday life, continuously greater expectations of flexibility and adaptability are directed towards every one of us, both in the shape of concrete claims from employers and colleagues, and, more subtle, as a part of the cultural atmosphere, the general social climate where the myth that "the world changes faster than ever" perhaps more than anything else stands at the service of the economic model power.

The ideal, both as it is carried forward in working life's basic ideas of continuous reorganising and life-long learning, and in the picture of the good life in "the world of things" in advertising and popular culture, is turned towards adjusting to constant change, playing with image, being continuously new and "not take oneself so seriously". The subject does not seem to be seen as a unity that mirrors itself in all its expressions and roles. In the late or postmodern working life and consumer culture, fragmentation and quick changes do not in themselves seem to be problematic. They are rather a necessity and for that matter also an ideal. In such a climate, responsibility will not easily gain a foothold.

It is one of the basic points of the French philosopher Michel

Foucault in his studies of power that the way society disciplines the human being is by transferring the constraints and ideals into us, so that they become a part of our own understanding and need structure. It is not a use of power that primarily pushes someone out of the good society, but rather a power that is integrated in the individual's self-conception – that defines the good and the desirable. Power has moved inside each and every one of us and becomes almost invisible, manifesting itself as our self-control.

The postmodern human being is constructed as a part of the necessity of society. It becomes social and compliant, a diligent consumer and an eager self-realising worker – continuously hunting for the new and pursuing its career (which is surprisingly similar to most others). Such a disciplinarian analysis of power consequently means that one emphasises the silent and non-dramatic, what almost imperceptibly slips in as a part of our own self-understanding and world view. Power works as the expectations we aim at ourselves, expectations which are often formulated in material terms or in terms of social status, consequently leading to some sort of economic action.

This is a relevant approach here since, as mentioned earlier in this chapter, one of my main statements is that traditional economic theory, by disregarding the formation of the preferences, seems badly equipped to grasp the fact that preferences can be influenced by power – and also by what we may refer to as illegitimate power. Something that we will have to say counts for at least part of the subtle exercise of the power of marketing and the fashion and life-style driven consumer culture. And this does not only apply at the micro level – by influencing the purchase of one label rather than another – it applies in the almost given desire for more consumption in general, as Arne Johan Vetlesen points out with a view to modern critical philosophy:

> It is all about power: someone's power and someone else's powerlessness. The philosopher Steven Lukes states it (not unlike

Marcuse) thus: "Is it not the ultimate exercise of power to make others want what you want them to want; that is, get their compliance by controlling their thoughts and wishes?" The result is a society where there is no difference between what the individual wants and what the society offers and points out as desirable: increased consumption, for instance.[125]

And as Siri Meyer emphasises: "Capitalism is like a huge machine of desire: it nourishes on social creatures' incessant recreation of identities, human beings that constantly name themselves. We cannot create an 'I' without consumer goods."[126] That the world comes forth to us more and more as an economic reality is, understood thus, an expression of a power that has no concrete executive force loosened from a message sent from any concrete sender. The powerful do not even need to recognize their own power, since they themselves are not necessarily aware of their dominant economic perspective of the world. The dialogical understanding of social responsibility that I have tried to bring up here is consequently meant to stimulate our consciousness of any such perspectivistic understanding, facilitating critique of what in several areas of society can be considered the hegemonic thinking of our time: the idea that we are primarily actors in an economic universe.

---

[125] In the article "Den lykkelige ubevissthet (Happy Unconsciousness)" in the Norwegian newspaper *Morgenbladet*, 7th July 2006. My translation from Norwegian.
[126] Meyer (2005, p. 32). My translation from Norwegian.

Chapter 6

# Summary and conclusion
Responsibility for what?

Not much can be as depressing in the public debate on CSR as when companies obviously disclaim or try to cover up their responsibility. When one spends millions on product branding that is supposed to include strong ethical qualities, a minimum of responsibility would of course be to actually tell the truth. A television programme on NRK (the Norwegian Broadcasting Corporation) recently revealed that Bama, importer and brand developer in Norway of the well-known "ethical" Bend-It (brand) bananas, clearly either did not know or did not sufficiently care about what actually happens at banana plants in several Latin American countries.[127] What was revealed was an almost classic case – including, among other things inexcusably low wages, poor and often dangerous working conditions and from the employers' side an active resistance to and sabotage of workers' attempts to establish unions.

With a "realistic attitude" toward social responsibility it therefore may seem as though we can not avoid the dualistic scheme between profitability and ethics: that we have to accept an analysis where

---

[127] NRK I, 23rd May 2006.

companies are primarily characterised by an intense will to obtain and make more money, at the same time as they generally seem to be developing a desire to keep their moral dignity and obtain the respect of the customers and the general public. Within such a realistic attitude, though, it always remains an open question where the line is drawn between real ethical business and just smart reputation management. It remains unclear what it indeed is one takes responsibility for.

In this book I have made an attempt to argue for and clarify how a call for more – and really ethical – social responsibility is related to something else, something larger than what is revealed in such depressing and classic business cases: that social responsibility is responsibility for society and not only for keeping business "clean". Whether we put company, household or individual as its prefix, responsibility applies to the social arrangement for a pluralistic extension and enrichment of our experiences in life as a whole, within the framework of a liberal, just and democratic social order. In our time this may mean that the economic sphere has to be restricted both locally and globally, and that we have to be substantially better in arranging for dialogue on what the basic goals of economic activities should be. Any desire for market solutions in an area of society is of course not the same as uncritical market liberalism, but any uncritical market liberalism is cultural pollution and an obstacle to individuals' free, autonomous development.

In such a picture the dualistic scheme is not valid. Nothing – nothing else than the discursive power of economic theory, that is – forces us to "realize" that economic realities equate profit with performance and ethics with (only) presentation. It is possible that "good ethics becomes good business when employees, customers, politicians and owners expect so, and when we deliver according to the expectations" as Svein Mollekleiv in the Norwegian company Det Norske Veritas recently wrote about business life and social responsibility.[128] But why always this turn back to profit? Why does this vulgar reductionism always lie there, floating, under often generally rich and enlightening ethical discussion? Ethics means exactly to *challenge, criticise and influence expectations* that create and recreate our social reality, rather than conforming to and answering them. The part of society that we give the tag economy does not contain obvious goals and measures that the rest of society has to be arranged in accordance with.

To justify responsibility for positive values in society with reference to an even more profitable business life is, strictly speaking, to turn our ethical reality upside down. The UN's Global Impact challenges international business life to contribute to the UN's millennium goal: the mantra is that "business will not succeed in a society that fails". This is obvious. Without, among other things, strong public institutions there can be no successful private markets in the long run. Something that is far from obvious, though, is what it actually means that a society succeeds. It can certainly not be reduced to the fulfilment of important conditions for industrial and commercial development – in that case one has been caught in a circular reasoning that is not philosophically tenable. A business life that supports the fight against poverty, the population's access to pure water, its right to education and better living conditions, because good business development will be difficult if they do not, is a perverted business life, a life with a corrupted understanding of responsibility.

Social responsibility is also a responsibility to keep the public dialogue open and alive. When economic thinking is becoming dominant, or hegemonic, the ethical attitude – that is the critical, free and radical disposition – resides in challenging the market fundamentalism that such thinking often brings, so that the dialogue on the eco-

---

[128] In a debate contribution in the Norwegian newspaper *Dagens Næringsliv*, with the title "Næringslivets ansvar" (The Responsibility of Business Life), 12th May 2006.

nomy and its part in the society can be conceptually rich and not reduced to instrumental reasoning alone. One has to search for the often implied assumptions that characterise the economic power and one way to do this is by proceeding empirically and asking how the market actually works. For economists and economy students who, like most other theoreticians, often orient themselves in the world based on idealised presumptions, this is particularly important when the dialogue is about when the market can actually be used as an efficient tool. Bent S. Tranøy presents five postulates made by the ones he calls market fundamentalists, and I want to cite these here as examples of matters that by being made objects for dialogue and challenged, rather than functioning as credos – professions of faith – can open the radical room of debate that is called for by addressing the concept of social responsibility:

1. *The chauvinistic postulate:* the private sector will always be better and more efficient that the public sector.
2. *The reductionistic postulate:* every product that human beings create can and should be realised in a market.
3. *The naturalistic postulate:* the market is the natural framework for economic co-action. Therefore markets are easily made.
4. *The circular justice-postulate:* what you get from a market reflects what you put in. Therefore the market is always just.
5. *The populistic postulate:* in a market it is the consumer that decides. The producers have to follow the consumer's wishes.[129]

The first postulate is mostly about the well-known division between private and public common goods in a society, a division that is not given, but that we have to make based on a political discussion of what should be regarded as different kind of values. The second

---

[129] Tranøy (2006, p. 25). My translation from Norwegian.

postulate is more radical and challenges us on the question of which goods that actually can be handled in a market, and which that are not first and foremost characterised by the private use value that can find its correct value in a market. The third points out that there will often be economic power relations that make it difficult to establish efficient market solutions, among others where production is based on expensive technology and consequently creates barriers for free entry. The forth focuses on things like succeeding based on luck rather that competence, and more basically whether the skills that lead to economic success are the ones that we would agree constitute human goodness and capability. The fifth and last postulate sets the agenda for the often hidden power mechanisms that can be manifested both within and outside the market, and that make us compliant and often less critical towards the prevailing ideology and to the icons of success that are carried with it.

These are postulates that, taken together, not only over-simplify the use of the market, but also imply an ideology that may reduce value pluralism in society. Accordingly, by challenging them we create not only consciousness about the practical difficulties of creating good and efficient markets but also stimulate an increased sensitivity to the non-economic value diversity that is in part what makes our economic actions meaningful. In this way the dialogue can generate the responsibility of us all for *not* making it accidental if the flow of money should graze the Good and the Beautiful, and that it sticks within the limits of the Right and the Just.

All these elements require a well-developed eye for the complex interaction between different institutions, values and ways of co-acting that keep society together. Let me therefore again cite Trangy when he says: "Too many, including well-educated and powerful people, have too little interest in thinking of and discussing the interaction between the constitutional state, bureaucracy, democracy, society, family and different shapes of market organising. Instead an oversimplified and idealised version of an organisation and motivation system is held up as the measure of everything."[130] In a time like ours, which is obviously a time for people of strong conviction – true believers – this delicate interaction is placed at the core of economic ethics. To counter economic power one has to move away from strong conviction and look for the social complexity and the multiplicity of values behind market solutions.

It is all about a) making the free market work efficiently b) where we want it and find it valuable to be working. And beneath all this lies always the personal question, a question that most clearly is also political, that, if asked seriously, challenges the whole growth systems we let run the economy today – namely the question of *what is enough?* Or to paraphrase Øystein Dahle in The Worldwatch Institute: Who is going to teach the joy of being able to manage with less? If the natural environment, our quality of life and ethics point in the direction of reduced consumption, how do we avoid just being driven in the opposite direction by an established system? The organising of the economy has to be a result of how large the economy needs to be, based on our needs and conditions for life, not what secures a system-defined and "necessary" growth. In acknowledging social responsibility lies the fact that it is painful to think – that it requires hard work to keep a steady, honest and critical eye on oneself and one's contribution to the way society develops.

The following simple sketch of different levels in our ethical consciousness on economic issues briefly summarises my position:

1. (Unethical) behaviour within business/the market economy.
2. The organisation and institutionalization of economic life.
3. The size of the economy (both related to ecological and cultural framework conditions, to our quality of and conditions for life).

[130] Tranøy (2006, p. 17). My translation from Norwegian.

A management perspective of corporate social responsibility gives priority to issues on level 1. The exposition in this book has hopefully given support to another view, where value issues on level 3 and 2 respectively are the most basic, and that the ethically correct is to let an open, proceeding dialogue on the size of and the organising of economic life be a determinant of our behaviour as economic actors. In the light of social responsibility, public and private life – politics, ethics and existentiality – are deeply intertwined.

# References

Aarnes, A.: "Den annens ansikt", *Inter Medicos*, no. 1, 1997, p. 14–19.
Aasland, D. G.: "Om grunnlaget for kritikken av markedsøkonomien", *Nytt Norsk Tidsskrift*, no. 2, 1999, p. 135–141.
Andersen, S.: "K. E. Løgstrups etikk", in ed.: A.J.Vetlesen, *Nærhetsetikk*, adNotam Gyldendal, 1996, p. 50–100.
Anderson, E.: *Values in Ethics and Economics*, Harvard University Press, 1993.
Asheim, I.: *Hva betyr holdninger? – Studier i dydsetikk*, Tano Aschehoug, 1997.
Bak, C.: *Det etiske regnskap – introduksjon, erfaringer og praksis*, Handelshøjskolens Forlag, 1996.
Bauman, Z.: *Postmodern Ethics*, Blackwell, 1996a.
Bauman, Z.: "Postmodernitet, identitet og moral", in ed.: A.J.Vetlesen, *Nærhetsetikk*, adNotam Gyldendal, 1996b.
Bernstein, R. J.: "Rorty's Inspirational Liberalism", in eds: C. Guignon/ D.R. Hiley, *Richard Rorty*, Cambridge University Press, 2003, p. 124–138.
Biong, Trine-L./Bu, K. (ed.): *Kunsten å være modig*, Flux Forlag, 2006.
Blackburn, S.: *Truth*, Oxford University Press, 2005.
Bowers, J./Mitchell, J./Lewis, J.: *Whistleblowing – The New Law*, Sweet and Maxwell, 1999.

Brytting, T.: *Företagsetik*, Liber, 1999.
Crane, A./Matten, D.: *Business Ethics – A European Perspective*, Oxford University Press, 2004.
Dahl, T.: "Havesyken som moralsk problem – er Adam Smiths løsning tilstrekkelig?", *Norsk Filosofisk Tidsskrift*, no. 3, 2002, p. 149–168.
De George, R. T.: *Business Ethics*, Pearson Prentice Hall, 6. utg, 2006.
Drucker, P. F: "What Is 'Busines Ethics'?", *The Public Interest*, vol. 63, 1981.
Ellwood, W.: "Dyster utvikling i økosystemet", *Friheten*, http://www.friheten.no/lang/2000/11/wayne.html.
Elsthain, J. B.: "Don't Be Cruel – Reflections on Rortyian Liberalism", in eds.: C. Guignon/D.R. Hiley, *Richard Rorty*, Cambridge University Press, 2003, p. 139–157.
Engelstad, F.: *Hva er makt?* Universitetsforlaget, 2005.
Eriksen, E. O./Weigård, J.: *Kommunikativ handling og deliberativt demokrati – Jürgen Habermas` teori om politikk og samfunn*, Fagbokforlaget, 1999.
Fenger-Grøn, C./Kristensen, J. E.: "Behovet for en kritikk av den økonomiske fornuft", in eds.: C. Fenger-Grøn/J. E. Kristensen, *Kritik af den økonomiske fornuft*, Hans Reitzels Forlag, 2001, p. 11–50.
Ferraro, F./Pfeffer, J./Sutton, R. I: "Economic language and Assumptions: How Theories Can Become Self-fulfilling", *Academy of Management Review*, no. 1, 2005, p. 8–24.
Forr, G.: "Bursdag på Rimi", *Dagbladet*, 21th July 2006.
Frankena, W. K.: *Ethics*, Prentice Hall, 1973.
French, P. A.: *Corporate Ethics*, Harcourt Brace, 1995.
Friedman, M.: "The Social Responsibility of Business Is to Increase Its Profits", *New York Times Magazine*, 13 sept., 1970.
Ghoshal, S.: "Bad Management Theories Are Destroying Good Management Practices", *Academy of Management Learning and Education*, no. 1, 2005, p. 75–91.
Gravelle, H./Rees, R.: *Microeconomics*, Longman, 1992.
Green, R. M.: *The Ethical Manager – A New Method for Business Ethics*, MacMillan, 1994.

Hansen, K. M.: "K.E. Løgstrups etikk og religionsfilosofi", in eds.: Kolstad/Aarnes, *Den etiske vending*, Aschehoug, 1996, p. 100–119.

Hegge, H.: *Frihet, individualitet og samfunn – en moralfilosofisk, erkjennelsesteoretisk og sosialfilosofisk studie i menneskelig eksistens*, Antropos, 2003.

Hellesnes, J.: *Illusjon?*, Samlaget, 2004.

Henriksen, J. O./Vetlesen, A. J: *Nærhet og distanse – grunnlag, verdier og etiske teorier i arbeid med mennesker*, Gyldendal akademisk, 2000.

Hesselbjerg, J.: "Den irrationelle rationalitet og den normative objektivitet", in eds.: C. Fenger-Grøn/J. E. Kristensen, *Kritik af den økonomiske fornuft*, Hans Reitzels Forlag, 2001, p. 249–270.

Jakobsen, O. D./Ingebrigtsen, S.: *Økonomi, natur og kultur*, Abstrakt Forlag, 2004.

James, P.: "Self-shaping Action", unpubl. (kilde: http://www.geocities.com/Athens/Delphi/2192/self.html)

Jensen, T. Ø.: "Forbrukerfølelser", in eds.: F. Nyeng/G. Wennes, *Kan organisasjoner føle?*, Cappelen Akademisk Forlag, 2005.

Kjeldsen, J. E.: *Retorikk i vår tid – En innføring i moderne retorisk teori*, Spartacus Forlag, 2004.

Klemsdal, L.: "Et inkluderende arbeidsliv? – om individualisering, organisasjon og dannelse av fellesskap i det nye arbeidslivet", in ed.: H. E. Nafstad, *Det omsorgsfulle mennesket – et psykologisk alternativ*, Gyldendal Akademisk Forlag, 2004, p. 118–149.

Kramvig, B.: Chronicle in *Bergens Tidende*, 18th December 1999.

Lambert, C.: "The Marketplace of Perceptions", *Harvard Magazine*. (source: http:www.harvardmagazine.com/on-line/030640.html)

Learned, E. P./Dooley, A. R./Katz, R. L.: "Personal Values and Business Decisions", *Harvard Business Review*, March-April, 1959, p. 111–120.

Lévinas, E.: *Etik og uendelighed*, Hans Reitzels Forlag, 1995.

Lévinas, E.: *Den annens humanisme*, Aschehoug, 1996.

Lie, T.: Editorial in *Morgenbladet*, 15th May 2001.

Lucas, J. R.: "The Responsibilities of a Businessman", in ed.: W. H. Shaw, *Ethics at Work*, Oxford University Press, 2003, p. 15–30.

Lundestad, E.: "Kan etikk og økonomi forenes?", *Magma – Tidsskrift for økonomi og ledelse*, no. 1, 2005, p. 77–84.

Lundestad, E.: Part IV: "Mennesket som sosialt vesen" of unnamed manuscript, unpubl., 2006.

Lunheim, K.: "Verdier, visjoner og kroner – beretningen om den etiske vekkelsen som hjemsøker vårt næringsliv", *Samtiden*, no. 3, 2005, p. 99–107.

Løgstrup, K. E.: *Kunst og etik*, Gyldendal, 1961.

Løgstrup, K. E.: *Norm og spontanitet*, Gyldendal, 1972.

Løgstrup, K. E.: *System og symbol*, Gyldendal, 1983.

MacIntyre, A.: *After Virtue – A Study in Moral Theory*, Duckworth, 1985.

Mahoney, J.: *Teaching Business Ethics in the UK, Europe and the USA*, The Athlone Press, 1990.

Marsdal, M. E./Wold, B.: *Tredje venstre. For en radikal individualisme*, Forlaget Oktober, 2004.

McIntosh, M./Thomas, R./Leipziger, D./Coleman, G.: *Living Corporate Citizenship – Strategic Routes to Socially Responsible Business*, Prentice Hall, 2003.

"Mer enn økonomi", *Morgenbladet*, 7th October 2005.

Meyer, S.: *Imperiet kaller – et essay om maktens anatomi*, Spartacus, 2003.

Meyer, S.: *Den lille Machiavelli – Maktspill til hverdagsbruk*, Aschehoug, 2005.

Nicolaisen, R. F.: *Å være underveis – Introduksjon til Heideggers filosofi*, Universitetsforlaget, 2003.

Nyeng, F.: *Etiske teorier – en systematisk fremstilling av syv etiske teoriretninger*, Fagbokforlaget, 1999.

Nyeng, F.: *Det autentiske menneske – med Charles Taylors blikk på menneskevitenskap og moral*, Fagbokforlaget, 2000.

Nyeng, F.: "Næringslivsetikk – besluttsomhetens kontra følsomhetens etikk", *Magma – Tidsskrift for økonomi og ledelse*, no. 3, 2002, p. 102–112.

Nyeng, F.: *Etikk og økonomi – en innføring*, Abstrakt Forlag, 2002.

Nyeng, F.: "Hva er en bedrift? – et verdipluralistisk næringslivsetikkperspektiv", in *Frihet og mangfold – festskrift til Odd G. Arntzen*, Tapir Forlag, 2003, p. 107–126.

Nyeng, F.: "Hvem tolker og hvem omfortolker? – konstruksjonen av økonomiske data i pragmatisk belysning, med vekt på forbrukerstudier", in eds.: Nyeng, F./Wennes, G., *Tall, tolkning og tvil – bak metodevalg i økonomi, ledelse og markedsføring*, Cappelen Akademisk Forlag, 2006, p. 23–68.

Nyeng, F.: "Bedrifter og samfunnsansvar – et pragmatisk perspektiv", *Magma – Tidsskrift for økonomi og ledelse*, no. 2, 2006, p. 88–100.

Næss, A.: *Livsfilosofi – Et personlig bidrag om følelser og fornuft*, Universitetsforlaget, 1998.

Orlando, J.: "The Ethics of Corporate Downsizing", in ed: W. H. Shaw, *Ethics at Work*, Oxford University Press, 2003, p. 31–48.

"Pragmatic Social Democrat" in *Morgenbladet*, October 7, 2005.

Primeaux, P.: "Business Ethics in Theory and Practice: Diagnostic Notes", *Journal of Business Ethics*, no. 3, vol. 16, 1997, p. 309–313.

Rasmussen, D. (ed.): *Universalism vs. Communitarianism*, The MIT Press, 1990.

Rorty, R.: *Contingency, Irony, and Solidarity*, Cambridge University Press, 1988.

Rorty, R.: *Objectivity, Relativism, and Truth – Philosophical Papers 1*, Cambridge University Press, 1991.

Rorty, R.: "Postmodernist Bourgeois Liberalism", in ed.: L. Menand, *Pragmatism – A Reader*, Vintage Books, 1997, p. 329–336.

Rosenberg, G.: *Plikten, profitten og kunsten å være menneske*, Flux Forlag, 2005.

Searle, J. R.: *Rationality in Action*, The MIT Press, 2001.

Sen, A.: *On Ethics and Economics*, Blackwell, 1987.

Skirbekk, G.: *Den filosofiske uroa – I spenninga mellom tvil og tru*, Universitetsforlaget, 2005.

Skjervheim, H.: *Deltakar og tilskodar og andre essays*, Aschehoug, 1996.

Solomon, R.: "Sosialt ansvar og etikk for næringslivet", in NHO-brochure *Marked og moral*, 1992.

Solomon, R.: *Ethics and Excellence: Cooperation and Integrity in Business*, Oxford University Press, 1993.

Solomon, R.: "Corporate Roles, Personal Virtues: An Aristotelian Approach to Business Ethics", in ed.: D. Statman, *Virtue Ethics – A Critical Reader*, Edinburgh University Press, 1997, p. 205–226.

Statman, D.: *Virtue Ethics – A Critical Reader*, Edinburgh University Press, 1997.

Svendsen, L.: "Er næringslivet dumhetens domene?", Samtiden, no. 3, 2001, p. 82–87.

"Ta det med ro" *Dagbladet*, 24th January 2006.

Taylor, C.: *PhilosophicalPpapers I*, Cambridge University Press, 1985a.

Taylor, C.: *Philosophical Papers II*, Cambridge University Press, 1985b.

Taylor, C.: *Sources of the Self – The Making of the Modern Identity*, Cambridge University Press, 1992.

*The New Atlantis – A Journal of Technology and Society*, 2006. http://www.thenewatlantis.com/archive/11/rosenprint.htm.

Thomassen, M.: "Etisk besinnelse", in *Embla*, no. 2, 1996.

Tranøy, B. S.: *Markedets makt over sinnene*, Aschehoug, 2006.

Varian, H. R.: *Microeconomic Analyses*, W.W Norton and Company, 1992.

Vetlesen, A. J: *Nærhetsetikk*, adNotam Gyldendal, 1996a.

Vetlesen, A. J: "Kommunitarisme", *Samtiden*, no. 4, 1996b.

Vetlesen, A. J./Henriksen, J-O.: *Moralens sjanser i markedets tidsalder – om kulturelle forutsetninger for moral*, Gyldendal Akademisk, 2004.

"Visjonshysteri i næringslivet", *Dagens Næringsliv*, 26th June 2006.

Wood, E. M.: *The Origin of Capitalism*, Monthly Review Press, 1999.

Wyller, T.: "Antikapitalismens ømme punkt?", *Agora*, no. 1-2, 2005, p. 219–232.